Stephen
Thank you!

Coralie —

You are a real beacon for

real beacon for

light in our community,

I am so thankful for

you. Much love!

Cath.

thank you!

THE AWAKENED COMPANY

THE
AWAKENED
COMPANY

CATHERINE R. BELL

IN COLLABORATION WITH **RUSS HUDSON**
AND **CHRISTOPHER PAPADOPOULOS**

namaste

PUBLISHING

Vancouver, Canada

Library and Archives Canada Cataloguing in Publication

Bell, Catherine R. 1971-, author
   The awakened company / Catherine R. Bell.

ISBN 978-1-897238-79-0 (bound)

   1. Business ethics. 2. Industrial management--Moral and ethical aspects. 3. Leadership--Moral and ethical aspects.
I. Title.

HF5387.B448 2015   174'.4   C2015-900502-7

Published in Canada by
NAMASTE PUBLISHING
P.O. Box 62084
Vancouver, British Columbia V6J 4A3
www.namastepublishing.com

Cover design by Diane McIntosh
Typesetting by Steve Amarillo / Urban Design
Printed and bound in Canada by Friesens

MIX
Paper from
responsible sources
FSC® C016245

DEDICATION

For all those who have felt listlessness,
disengagement, fear, anger, frustration, and
pain in their work within organizations.
And for the love of my life, Kent Brown, and
our sons John and Michael, who have my
heart in their hands.

Readers, you now have our
minds and hearts in your hands.
Thank you for choosing this book.

CONTENTS

ACKNOWLEDGMENTS

Above all, I want to thank my husband Kent Brown, and my sons, John and Michael, who supported and encouraged me in spite of all the time it took me away from them. Thank you to my aunt, Ruth Tait, who was an endless fountain of inspiration. Thank you to my mother, Pam Bell, and my father in the sky, Tom Bell. This is for my sons, nieces, nephews, sisters (Kim Bell, Jen Bell, and Tori Brown), Sam Fryer, brothers-in-law (Jeff, Wes, Grant, and Blake), MIL, FIL, cousins, aunts, uncles, and godchildren.

It was a mercurial and non-linear journey. I would like to express my gratitude to all those who provided support and saw me through this book, specifically my colleagues Carolyn Duckworth, Bryan Arthur, Sarah Hawitt, Shahauna Siddiqui, Dianne Aronyk, Bliss Aime, Nicole Dixon, Hilary Lungu, Tamara Cohos, Julie Kemp, and the entire team at BluEra—and thank you to all who talked things over, read, wrote, offered comments, allowed me to quote their remarks, and assisted in the editing, proofreading, and design, particularly Amanda Graves for her detailed review. Thanks too to Corinne Hamilton for the photo she took of me—it was a fun afternoon.

Thank you to my yoga instructors Francesca Ter Poorten and Jennifer Anderson. Thank you also to all my clients, connection with whom has proven invaluable for the writing of this book. You rock! Thank you Flemming Christensen for hosting our first international event. Further, I must also thank Nilda Mallon for always ensuring our home is organized (no easy feat), which enabled a clearer environment to write in, as well as Paul Zelizer for relentless support and encouragement. Thank you to the cities of Calgary, Alberta (especially the 7th Street support team and Elbow Park posse); Santa Fe, New Mexico; Montreal, Quebec; New York, NY; and Cabo, San Lucas; as well as Fernie, British Columbia, and cottage country, for holding the space for this journey. Thank you to my amazing spiritual book club.

My collaborators, Russ Hudson and Chris Papadopoulos, I deeply value your insightful comments that helped to bring *The Awakened Company* to life.

I wish to thank Namaste Publishing for publishing this book. Constance Kellough, your relentless love and support has meant the world to me. Bob Brown, thank you for introducing me to Constance, which led to publication of *The Awakened Company*. Thank you to Lucinda Beacham for her detailed work. I would sincerely like to thank my editor at Namaste Publishing, David Robert Ord, for his ability to weave magic into the original manuscript.

To all those teams willing to risk the journey into awakening, I wish you oodles of rewarding experiences. Deep bow to you, the reader, who will deepen and bring the material to life.

— Catherine R. Bell

1

THE BOOM-BUST BIPOLARITY
OF THE BUSINESS WORLD

The presumption that work is separate from the rest of
life, and therefore operates under different rules, has been
widely taken for granted since the dawn of the modern economy. It's so ingrained in our work practices, that we don't normally question it. We assume it's just "how things are," as if the
way businesses operate was akin to natural laws like gravity.

At the root of our economic mindset is the axiom "business is business." This statement assumes that the purpose
of business is to make money, and whatever it takes to do so
is okay—as long as it's legal, at least quasi-legal, or can be
gotten away with. While few would admit this publicly, it's
tacitly assumed by most people, both inside and outside the
business world. This statement also assumes that how things
have been is the only way they can be. Yet, few today would
argue that "business as usual" is working well.

The financial crisis of 2007 through 2009, in which in
the United States alone 8.8 million jobs were lost and $19.2
trillion in household wealth vanished,[1] has given the lie to
the deeply entrenched belief that "business is just business,"
separate from the rest of life—as did the Enron scandal

before it, along with the subsequent financial improprieties of the likes of JPMorgan Chase and Goldman Sachs. Beyond the ethical issues these situations raise, the values that precipitated these scandals are rapidly undermining, and in some cases destroying, the very economic system in which they are operating.

This book draws on solid data to challenge the idea that business can be conducted separately from the rest of life and achieve sustained success. This data points in a diametrically opposite direction from many of the common assumptions and principles by which businesses function and on which economies are founded.

For instance, the thrill of rapid growth and expansion into wider markets, especially international markets, drives many modern businesses. On the way up, seeing the sky as the limit, few in these businesses question what's being sacrificed in the pursuit of relentless growth driven by a "profit is everything" mentality. On the way down, employees experience increasing stress as they realize the job they counted on to fund their home purchase, new car, medical insurance, and college tuition for their kids is threatened—and, in many cases, their retirement. As the company loses its direction and profit margins tank, they watch helplessly while management close ranks trying to protect their own positions and wealth. No one is ready when the floor gives way and layoffs follow, not to mention the devastating effect such collapses have on local economies.

Why do we assume that to increase shareholder value is of utmost importance to businesses, when the reality is that increasing shareholder value benefits the few, not the majority? In contrast, innovation in the marketplace, improving the wellbeing of the community in which the business functions, and making decisions for the longevity of the company and its team are much more relevant. Setting the context for awakening involves allowing others to own their giftedness and step into their strengths, whereas presently the focus of companies is primarily on "hiring" a "workforce" for growth. We are talking about the entire team functioning in a context in which each member of the team "comes into their own" in a fulfilling, creative life that blends harmoniously with the whole of individuals' lives. In those companies that have already shifted into this mode of operation, the financial rewards for the leadership, the team, and the shareholders have been substantial— not to forget the value to the community.

It's crucial to understand that the fact there are financial rewards isn't the reason to make such a change. They are merely the spinoff. A team I have been working with the last few years has seen their revenues increase over 80%. But what's ultimately meaningful is that their enjoyment of the work and the relationships involved has become truly satisfying.

The boom-bust bipolarity of the modern marketplace has consequences not only for the economy as a whole, but also for those who are at the helm of businesses that are experiencing this roller coaster. In too many cases, it has led to disaster and destruction for the firm itself, as well as for most who were associated with it. Levels of dissatisfaction, and in many cases downright depression, have risen right along with the drop in profitability.[2] Parallel with this, the middle class—the basis of every healthy economy—has been shrinking rapidly in many developed countries. The factors leading up to this were in evidence well before the crash of 2008, and the malaise of that crash still lingers.

The global economic situation is at an impasse. Everyone recognizes that "business as usual" not only isn't cutting it, but is becoming increasingly difficult to sustain. Too many businesses are focused on individual wealth, mostly for upper management, along with the generation of profit for stockholders. Little thought is put into the long-term consequences for employees, let alone society as a whole.

This boom-bust bipolarity has particularly eroded public confidence in the corporate sector. When a corporation's instinct is to activate a massive PR campaign instead of showing deep remorse and making true amends for their violations, a sense of disgust grows among the population. Given the disastrous effects wreaked on society by some companies—and the near silence of the rest of the business community, which amounts to tacit support for such behavior—it isn't difficult to understand the public's anger and lack of trust in the current business model. People from diverse walks of life have come to the conclusion that many corporations are evil and need to be fought and stopped. At the very least, it has become obvious to almost everyone that the historic notions of doing business are rapidly unraveling on nearly all levels.

The Travesty of Meaningless Work

Public awareness of the widespread corruption leading up to the financial crash of 2008 helped to speed up this change of attitude towards the world of work. The colossal global problems this crash created exposed many of the old assumptions about business that are long overdue for revision. The events of recent years have especially caused many members of the workforce to seriously reflect on their employment—and indeed their lives in general. They are realizing that a large slice of their daily existence is committed to something that doesn't fulfill them. Not only do they not enjoy what they are doing, but it takes them away from loved ones and denies them pursuit of their passion.

A growing number are asking, "Is there a connection between a stressful, unfulfilling work environment and the financial struggle I experience from pay check to pay check? What is the work I do all day really about? What's the point of it all? Does the company on which I rely for my livelihood really have to engage in high risk behavior, potentially sweeping away my pension and perhaps even my job? What's stopping us from building a fulfilling work environment that's rewarding for everyone?"

Rather than simply being angry at the system and going to work in a disgruntled state each day, I propose that the current discontent is an invitation to find a solution. By "solution," I'm referring not only to the plight of multitudes in the labor force, but also the stress suffered by many business owners who are more than ever feeling the weight of the world on their shoulders as they wrestle with issues such as health care, while being blamed for the economic, environmental, and social problems of today. Both owners and people who work with them need to feel that what they do is serving real needs, not hyped needs—needs that are purpose and value driven. All involved then feel they are contributing something meaningful instead of simply earning a pay packet.

In the midst of all this turmoil, something profound is happening. In the wake of the wreckage of businesses, communities, and families—all of which are suffering from the effects of the current economic paradigm—a number of prominent companies are beginning to see how expediency and short-sightedness, which for some time have been the norm, are failing us. There is a growing realization that, with every decline, the boom-bust cycle weakens the foundations of our economy and thereby militates against our ability to build a prosperous future for all.

With this realization, these companies are discovering a different way of doing business, and in the process providing us with solid evidence that there really *is* another—a better—way of structuring the world of work.

Business Is Community

There was a time not so long ago when it was natural for companies to grow out of families and partnerships among people with similar skills and interests. They were an organic part of our society's sacred economic trinity: family, community, and business. Businesses were explicitly part of communities and recognized their reciprocal relationship with the people they served.

Being part of the community meant companies felt more responsible for their employees' wellbeing, since these employees were also neighbors. Employees were recipients of an apprenticeship model that passed on the skills, values, and vision of this economic community within the wider community. Such an environment encouraged both individual confidence and a spirit of collaboration.

As corporations expanded beyond local communities, the sense of being neighbors working together for the good of the community was increasingly sacrificed to a business model based on profit for shareholders who had no investment in the communities from which labor was drawn. Consequently, instead of being answerable to the community, companies today are primarily answerable to a CEO whose chief concern is to meet the expectations of those with a financial investment at stake.

Dr. Harish Hande,[3] founder and managing director of Selco Solar, a social enterprise developed to eradicate poverty through sustainable technologies in rural India, believes that the current understanding of who a company's stakeholders are is far too limited and that it goes far beyond the shareholders. He sees a need for a paradigm shift in terms of leadership—a shift away from the competitive model that currently drives commerce. He confesses, "I want a really different model of leadership today."

While there is much we can learn from these former ways of doing business, we also recognize we are in a different situation now. We may well rediscover some of the values that drove those earlier forms of community-based businesses. However, we also need to include the many variables that the modern global economy brings into the picture. Restoring balance to the global economy will require both business students and leaders to rethink the present corporate culture because the roots of the present system are dying. It's time to plant the seeds for a new forest that yields much healthier, higher quality, long-term growth that benefits everyone. This means thinking *holistically*, as well as in terms of *interactive systems*.

What this implies is outlined by Dr. Hande, who explains, "One always hears from the business world—'to increase the value for shareholders.' This is a lopsided statement. What businesses should really work towards is 'to increase the value for *all* stakeholders, which includes end-users, employees, management and shareholders.'"[4] We incorrectly assume that "maximizing shareholder value" is the key business mantra. The facts show that nothing could be further from the truth. This mantra causes share buy-backs, offshoring of manufacturing, and the destruction of communities.

Mac Van Wielingen,[5] co-chair of ARC Financial, chairman of ARC Resources, and president of Viewpoint Capital, defines corporate culture as how we treat one another, which includes how we relate to the multitude of stakeholders. Do we treat our true stakeholders with respect?

Van Wielingen's understanding of "stakeholders" includes our employees, customers, suppliers, competitors, the communities and countries in which we operate, the earth and its creatures, as well as those who invest in our company financially.

Van Wielingen believes that when we discover *everyone* is a stakeholder in our business, we will all prosper.

Otto Scharmer,[6] Senior Lecturer at MIT and Founding Chair of the Presencing Institute, sums up, "It's basically a journey from 'me to we' or a journey from 'ego to eco,' a mindset that's focusing on not only my own wellbeing but the wellbeing of the whole, the wellbeing of all others."

Craig Kielburger,[7] cofounder of Me To We, echoes this. "It sounds idealistic," he admits, "but success is shifting the world—and we even say shifting consciousness—from me to we."

Echoing and expanding on this, internationally renowned author and academic Henry Mintzberg[8] believes that business leaders need to modify their understanding of leadership to set the stage for the emergence of what he calls "communityship."

It's important to grasp how fundamentally different the concept of communityship is from what leadership in the business world has come to mean for most of us. A shift from our current understanding of leadership, which tends to reside in an individual such as the CEO of a company, to businesses based on communityship involves *recapturing the sense we are all neighbors sharing the planet.*

Articulating this difference, Mintzberg explains, "The mindset has become so obsessively leadership oriented that every time anybody uses the word 'leadership,' they mean an individual. Company efforts aren't about individuals. They are about people working together. So we need an understanding of leadership as something that caters to communityship. It's perhaps different in entrepreneurial companies, where one person is really setting the tone and getting things started. But once the company is established, it's a matter of managing it as a community."

What might a business built on communityship look like? SELCO's Dr. Harish Hande explains, "You don't feel you have to win and the other person has to lose. Instead, you work collaboratively toward a shared vision around values stakeholders care about. For instance, we all need to care about the planet we live on, which requires cleaning up our act personally and as a company. It's a matter of being conscious."

The term "conscious" is an interesting one, in that at first glance it might appear we are all already conscious. Yet when we look more closely, it becomes apparent that much of what we do is either rote or only partially informed by facts. A great deal of the time, we operate with only partial awareness of all the factors required to make truly intelligent decisions. Governed more by habit and the status quo than by a thorough grasp of the realities of a situation, we tend to do much of what we do on autopilot. The field of Social

Psychology is using the latest brain research showing that what G. I. Gurdjieff[9] said is true—almost all of our so-called decisions are not conscious at all, but are more in the line of automatic impulses from past conditioning in the brain.

How it's possible to be a conscious human being, while at the same time largely unaware, can be seen from the way that, perhaps even daily, many of us drive to and from work in a rote manner, with little awareness of where we actually are on our journey. When a greater degree of awareness kicks in, we suddenly find ourselves noticing this and asking, "Oh, did I pass the gas station yet?" or, "Did I miss my turn?" Instead of being fully aware—truly present in the act of driving—we realize we were lost in thought.

Thankfully, we can learn to be more awake—to notice such distractions more often and more quickly, and to return our attention to the matter at hand. We can do this as individuals, and we can also create relationships and groups in which focusing our attention becomes more the norm.

Toward Awakened Companies

Often we refer to a company as if it's a distinct entity from the people in it, when, in fact, its very existence is dependent entirely on us as human beings. Without people, there *is* no company.

A corporation that thinks of itself as an entity is really working more with legal and mental concepts than reality. Oddly, this has become the normal way of thinking of companies. Our society creates corporations, which we then protect as legal entities, leading us to forget that it's simply humans who create, develop, and support all businesses. Without us, the corporation cannot act, feel, or think. On its own, devoid of humans, it's just a concept.

Companies are nothing more than human beings who have agreed to function together, and no organization exists but for the actions and choices of the human beings of which it's comprised. For this reason, the degree of awareness of the individuals in the company, as well as the quality of their relationships, is critical for the intelligent functioning of that company. Whether such companies are what we refer to in this book as "awakened" is the question at hand. One indicator of an awakened company is whether it operates for the good of all, or whether what it does has side effects that are harmful to its workers, its clients, the wider community, and the environment.

Said differently, companies are human communities. If we once begin to think of our places of work not as something divorced from the rest of life, but as communities that are a vital dimension of our existence as people, and in fact at the heart of a meaningful life, a fundamentally different idea of how a company should operate enters the picture.

The knowledge that it is *people* who create economic success, and also people who are responsible for economic crises, implies that these same individuals might be capable of imagining and creating other kinds of business models that don't swing between boom and bust. As a number of powerful and successful companies are already demonstrating, we need not be "passive victims" to structures that no longer serve our purposes.

By paying attention to companies that are thriving, along with learning from past mistakes of companies such as Enron, or the "dot com bust," and the financial crisis of 2007-2009, we will see that we already possess the ability to transform our businesses into communities that bring sustained prosperity to growing numbers of people in a manner that harms no one, including the planet itself. This becomes possible as such businesses essentially regard the entire human race as their extended family, which would constitute a return to the more personal and community based business model that was originally rooted in families, albeit with an expanded awareness of global participation and impact.

The paradigm shift we are talking about is, from one vantage point, huge. Yet, from another perspective, it's an extremely small shift. The reality is, it doesn't take as much as we might think to make a vast difference in the quality of people's lives. Indeed, quite small decisions and changes in behavior can greatly affect our businesses and society as a whole for the better—far more so than is generally acknowledged.

In many companies, executives and employees alike are taking a hard look at themselves, and in the process finding a truer calling. Changing their metrics for "success," they are discovering that it's not the flashiness of our cars, the size of our homes, or the fatness of our wallets that are the real barometer of "the good life." While none of these things are bad in and of themselves, more and more intelligent people are realizing that these traditional signifiers of success generally don't lead to a sense of meaning or purpose, let alone fulfillment. Rather, what many are discovering, and what some of the studies you will see in this book readily back up, is that what really makes for a rich life is the degree of our awareness, the depth of our relatedness, the wellness of our communities, and the overall quality of life enjoyed by *all* who dwell on our planet.

A Different Business Model

While the majority of companies are asleep at the switch and operating largely in a state of oblivion with regard to the real situation of our world today, a growing number of companies are in different stages of waking up. This awakening isn't some kind of fringe movement. On the contrary, it may come as a surprise to learn which well-known successful companies are undergoing deep transformation that reverses the "business is business" mantra. We will be introducing you to several of them whose executives we have personally interviewed.

A company engaging in this process of transformation is what I call an "awakened" company. Why "awakened"? To be awake is to possess awareness, whether as a company or as an individual—or what we earlier referred to as "consciousness." To be awake is to be explicitly aware of what's going on around us and within us. Like anything worthwhile in life, this awareness is a capacity that develops and improves as we practice using it. We are in the process of awakening.

To be awake as a company means to behave in a manner that reflects our understanding that no individual or entity exists in isolation from anyone or anything else. Everything that exists is interrelated and interactive. Thus, an awakened company is aware of the reality of its dependence upon and connection with the context in which it functions—a context that includes its employees, the wider human community that supports it, and the natural environment from which it draws its resources.

Companies are awake to the extent that they recognize they are nested within other structures as part of a richly interconnected matrix, and make their policy and operational decisions based on that awareness. In contrast, much like an individual ego, companies have their eyes shut to the extent they think and behave as if they were independent of larger contexts and relationships.

As executives and as companies, we can be more or less awake, which means that, even with good intentions, we may or may not notice when we are taking a path that's going to ultimately prove self-destructive. One could say that our capacity to make intelligent decisions is directly related to our level of awareness. This applies to groups as well as to individuals. Further, our degree of awareness isn't fixed, but can fluctuate countless times, even in a single day. The trick is to learn to be sufficiently awake to notice these fluctuations. There could be a group working together, an entire organization, or simply two people relating to each other, all with different levels of awareness.

Once we *really* wake up—really grasp the interdependent nature of life—we realize that a company must exist to serve our interconnectedness as much as it exists to make a profit. This is a fundamentally different understanding of business than the traditional view of such organizations as primarily profit-generating machines. Awakening businesses are no longer aligned with the limiting belief that "business is business." Instead, they are increasingly integrating their business life into the rest of life.

In line with this, Jeffrey Pfeffer and Robert Sutton in *Hard Facts, Dangerous Half Truths & Total Nonsense* comment, "The bad news is that the presumption that work is separate and operates under different rules than the rest of life is widely taken for granted. It is so ingrained in so many work practices that it does massive and widespread damage." These authors go on to say, "By challenging this half-truth with solid data and logic and then borrowing, inventing, and experimenting with practices that weave together rather than segregate and tear apart our different roles, there are bright prospects for both progress and performance."[10]

No matter how large and internationally based any business may become, its ability to function depends on the communities in which it operates, from which it draws its resources and labor, and that are its clients. When a business recognizes its utter dependence on community, and in line with this fosters community within its own interior structure, it sets itself apart from the bipolar boom-and-bust economy. It prepares itself to become not only profitable, but beneficial, sustainable, and enduring. The multidimensional health of people—mental, physical, emotional, relational, financial— and ongoing corporate wellbeing are balanced.

2

REWIRING THE NETWORK

Once we realize we are all in the economic matrix together, it becomes apparent how much of our wellbeing is based on relationships, both those we recognize and those of which we are usually unaware.

You can see this by simply looking at the clothes you are wearing or considering where your last meal originated. Who conceived of these things, designed them, produced them, transported them, opened the relevant warehouses and stores, and assembled the necessary staff to make them available to you? And where did you obtain the financial resources to purchase these items, let alone the car in which you drove to the store (or the public transport), and the closet and refrigerator in which to store your acquisitions? Each of these seemingly discrete items is actually the product of a long chain of interdependence. This might be hard to accept for the narcissistic parts of ourselves that want to believe we "did it all ourselves," but it doesn't take any exceptional awareness to see just how deeply we are embedded in interrelated human activities and relationships.

In the business world as we presently know it, there's a predominance of linear thinking. As a result, too many strategic plans, not to mention funds, sit on the sidelines, often on bookshelves, when what's needed is a focus on what the present moment is asking of us in light of the longer term vision. Life and organizations don't function in a linear manner. For example, a valued employee suddenly leaves. A new leader takes charge, promoting a different vision. An unexpected service line emerges. Such changes have a way of torpedoing typical strategic plans on which teams have spent countless hours, all for naught.

We tend to think of the linear approach as masculine, with the boardroom as its epitome. Sadly, however, this approach has seeped into just about every area of life. It may surprise you to hear that linear thinking manifests even in yoga groups that are comprised mainly of women! For example, the downward dog pose is typically performed in an angular, linear fashion. This pose naturally invites you to sway your hips, roll back your shoulders, arch your spine, and curve your calves in order to integrate more of the fluid, circular mode of the feminine. The serious imbalance between linear and non-linear needs to be redressed, with both being implemented as need arises.

If we truly begin to think about our lives, it quickly becomes clear that, in a modern economy especially, we can't even survive, let alone thrive, apart from a vast network of enterprises. In countless ways that are seen and unseen, the modern world involves people taking care of themselves by caring for the needs of others.

At some level, most of us recognize we need community just to exist, let alone to innovate and prosper. Yet, it seems it's often only in times of disaster that this awareness rises into full consciousness. For instance, I was in the flood of 2013 in Calgary. Because the pressure was on, a higher conscious-ness manifested itself spontaneously as people did what was required to be done. It was unplanned, emergent, community based, and had an energy of its own. Those who were in New York on 9/11 and in the days that followed might well remem-ber a similar phenomenon. Organization was based on what needs had arisen, a model for how all organizations need to rise to what's needed. This is the key to fulfilling what's "real" in the economy, instead of hyped needs.

In his book *On Servant Leadership*,[1] Robert Greenleaf rightly emphasizes the need to serve other people. While I agree with the importance of serving, it's also the case that some of us fall into the trap of "give, give, give," since service has become our mantra. I believe that it's equally essential to focus on what's most needed in the moment. For example, instead of taking action when action isn't really needed at this moment, the wise choice might be to sleep on a decision. The research shows that when people are properly rested, they tend to make smarter decisions that are more in tune with the demands of a situation.

Imagine if we could access this kind of awareness without requiring a disaster to induce it. This is where we begin to see how the development of awareness makes new choices possible. If it's true we need each other—even though, most of the time, most of us are unaware of our interconnectedness and interdependence—how much more might we all benefit if, instead of working *against* one another, we actually began to work *with* one another in a conscious manner?

While many people might feel they would rather work with others than against them, the unconscious habits we have accumulated through our history, both individual and collective, make it difficult to act on this more creative impulse in a sustained way. However, by noticing our habits and making them conscious, we empower ourselves to convert an idea that sounds good into a practical, lived reality. This accomplishes the life-altering shift from seeing the other as an opponent to realizing that, beyond sheer survival, we cannot thrive without each other—an insight that invites a massive restructuring of our economies, along with the corporations, companies, and businesses that comprise them.

Why "Going with the Flow" Is Crucial in Business

The profoundly different sense of ourselves and our connection to the whole of life to which this book points is something we literally *feel*, as our mind stops chattering, our emotional turmoil quiets down, our physical body loses its tenseness, and our voice becomes relaxed instead of strained. In this more awakened state, we find ourselves more grounded, more emotionally connected, and experience an alertness and clarity that facilitate an openness in which creativity begins to flow, as from a life-giving spring.

Working *with* the flow of life instead of against it—*with* the universe and its natural resources, seeing them as a gift rather than regarding them as something to be conquered—opens up a vista of possibilities that transcend our present vision.

For instance, if we were to question whether our prolonged exploitation of and reliance on fossil fuels may be jeopardizing our children's future, relaxing into a deeper awareness—and thus engaging the flow of our creative genius—would allow us to relinquish our ego's attachment to the wealth and benefits derived from fossil fuels thus far. As we learn how beneficial and intelligent this flow of awareness is, applying it to our lives as we go, we come to trust it more. Consequently, it isn't such a big jump to embrace the many changes before us. Trusting the beneficence of the interdependent nature of reality, we would then open ourselves to wherever the creative flow may wish to take us next, having full confidence that it will be an advance on our present situation—not a step back toward the Stone Age, as so many often object based on their fears.

Creativity can never be about resistance. It always presages new horizons, which is why it can't be fossilized.

Companies and governments that seek to hold onto "how we've always done things," instead of opening to a new paradigm, are cut off from the essential creativity these times require and are thus doomed to failure—and, if allowed to continue in their entrenched ways, may doom us all through their disastrous practices. We can look at history or our own lives and see that whenever we turned away from the invitation to explore new possibilities, clinging to what was at a certain point a necessary stage of our evolution and resisting innovation needed for the next stage, we put our very survival at risk.

A Smart Way to Open Up New Frontiers in Business

The basic shift called for is one in which we view our businesses—or any other organizations, for that matter—as an ongoing process of learning and developing practices that ground the learning.

When our mindset is one of inquiry, we deepen our ability to investigate in ways heretofore undreamed of. As we become more receptive to new possibilities in our ourselves and in others, we find ourselves increasingly free to act in ways unfamiliar to our habitual sense of ourselves. We are awakening to our potential for creativity and more beneficial ways of doing things—in other words, to a fresh understanding of what it means "to be in business."

When our learning is understood in the context of an awareness of our ultimate interdependence in our dealings with one another, we see all our interactions as an interchange of sacred communication and appreciation. What has until now been a mere coincidental sharing of a planet at a particular time in its history is transformed by seeing each other as human beings who are learning together, and whose lives are intrinsically interwoven in countless ways at a deep level.

As we begin to recognize those we have business dealings with as people like ourselves, we move beyond our habitual competitiveness into a new understanding of humanity as a collective expression of an evolving global intelligence. We can then begin to work with other awareness-oriented individuals toward shared goals. Functioning from this intelligence, we become capable of great insight and even genius, which facilitates entirely fresh and exciting new approaches to the kinds of challenges that arise when using the earth's resources, harnessing its energy, and working together as a species for the greater good.

The way forward is to turn the light of introspection on our business enterprises and the way our companies and governments are structured. When we do so, we discover previously unknown assets in our existing personnel, hidden opportunities in our changing circumstances, and untapped prosperity that can transform the lives of all who journey with us on spaceship earth.

The Brain Rewires Itself

Science has revealed that the process of developing deeper awareness and awakening to an enlarged sense of ourselves, accompanied by an expanded understanding of the businesses in which we are engaged, triggers a restructuring in our brain. We find ourselves undergoing an actual physical *rewiring* of our neural circuits based on our different thinking, our ability to feel more deeply, and a growing capacity to act in innovative ways.

The more our understanding of ourselves gets stretched—along with our understanding of those we work with and what our business is really all about—the more our brain literally disconnects old circuits based on ego, freeing us to see ourselves, others, and situations in ways yet undreamed of. As the relatively new science of neuroplasticity compels us to realize, in terms of the work we perform, we in effect engage in our own conscious evolution as a person, a team, and a company.

Many of our old mental and behavioral patterns may have been useful at one point, but our overreliance on them can cause us to forget that more spontaneous, creative, and intelligent parts of us are available when we are more aware. It's important we learn to be aware of such patterns so that our native intelligence doesn't get blunted by their habitual nature.

Whereas our potential has in so many cases been stunted by outdated thinking and patterns of behavior programmed into us years ago—and at the corporate level, often decades or even centuries ago—tapping into our ability to respond in fresh, wiser, and more compassionate ways actively *reshapes our brain*, thereby gifting us with opportunities to reimagine and reshape the businesses we constitute.

Specifically, as a recent study reveals, to train ourselves

to observe our tendency to react, along with developing the mental muscle to ground ourselves and contain our reactions instead of acting them out, triggers significant changes in those regions of the brain associated with self-awareness, memory, stress, and empathy.[2]

Becoming more acutely aware, which is a foundational dimension of an awakened state, is also known to strengthen our prefrontal lobe, which helps us be more ethical, compassionate, insightful, and intuitive—and at the same time less anxious, depressed, fearful, and impulsive.[3]

In addition, we become better at reasoning, planning, and detecting errors—in effect, better problem solvers and decision makers, and therefore ultimately better human beings capable of not just imagining but actually creating a better world. In short, developing awareness may be the most practical thing we ever do!

An Invitation to Move Beyond Our Present Limitations

Another important element of the awakened state is that we no longer see most issues in terms of black or white. Instead, we are able to appreciate many perspectives on a matter—the black, the white, and the infinite shades of gray in between these polarities. When we hold a black-or-white view of things, it tends to be because we've been conditioned to hold onto a set of historic opinions, both negative and positive. To see the wider perspective requires us to release our cherished opinions and recognize what's actually relevant here and now.

It's a process of becoming *present*—something an expanding slice of the business world is keen to do, while other parts of the world of commerce fight it tooth and claw.

The alternative to working from the limitations of our established patterns of thinking and acting is to enter into an open field of energy, increasingly unencumbered by past identifications, projections, or habits, such as the way we have historically seen ourselves, or what psychologists call our "self-image." We often imbue our self-concept with our sense of worth, so we naturally feel defensive about it. This is why, whenever we come from our self-image, we tend to see issues as if our viewpoint were the only one that's truly valid. Such a narrow approach to our business life can cause us to be resistant to new ideas and changes, or at best overly cautious and conservative, with the result that we miss the ambiguous nature of countless situations—miss the many subtle but critically important elements. Instead of seeing the potential in exploring different avenues, we latch onto a strategy based either on our habitual way of approaching matters or on our previous experiences, thereby becoming relics of the past.

When we view an issue from a more open perspective, the appropriate response in any given situation no longer appears set in concrete. In this more open mode, we are more likely to see things as they actually are, untainted by our personal biases, the prejudices of others, or what has always been considered "company policy." As we become less attached to our old points of view, we are able to bring more objectivity to our work. Less subjective in our view of things, we become more realistic.

As we deal with situations as they actually *are*, the horizon expands. Giving our full attention to the reality before us, we don't waste energy on clashing personal viewpoints that are wrapped up in "company policy" or "company tradition," but that have little relevance to the actual situation as it is in the present. Instead, we allow *this* situation to unfold, *this* moment to be exactly what it is, untainted by our biases or fantasies and free to flow toward a heretofore unimagined destiny.

As our tendency to either divert or dam up the flow of creativity recedes, and we no longer resist the unknown, previously unseen and even unimagined solutions to present obstacles have a way of coming into view.

3

THE CENTRALITY OF
THE COMPANY CULTURE

"Good ideas supported by the wrong culture seldom gain full value when implemented," concludes a course by Cornell Advanced Program for Executive Search Consulting. On the other hand, "Average ideas implemented with a supportive culture often provide strong results."[1]

For this reason, concludes the report, "Culture trumps planning."

To Tony Hsieh,[2] CEO of Zappos, such a finding comes as no surprise. "Our number one priority is company culture," he says. "Our whole belief is that if we get the culture right, then most of the other stuff like delivering great customer service or building a long-term, enduring brand or business will be a natural byproduct of the culture."

Even though a corporate culture involves many elements, it can be detected in all the individuals in the company. It's seen in their values, norms of behavior, expectations, rituals, myths, relationships, physical space, sounds, and rewards—anything touching on how a company's personnel work together.

A healthy company culture recognizes the truth of Albert Einstein's words, "What a person does on his own, without being stimulated by the thoughts and experience of others, is even in the best of cases rather paltry and monotonous." However, a company culture isn't just about individuals , working together to produce more than they could alone. When a company functions as a true community, the result is greater than the sum of its parts.

Developing a Healthy Culture

At a January 2013 Institute for Corporate Directors event on strategy, held in Calgary, Canada, I heard a quote from Peter Drucker that "corporate culture eats strategy for lunch." Yet in the world of business, how much is invested in strategic planning compared with investment in culture development? There is fear around culture development. Why? Because it's the nonlinear side of business, which is more challenging to measure. It's the softer aspect, which terrifies many of us. Corporate culture is the mercurial secret sauce of business and represents the more awakened energy.

Culture can trump egoic leadership, which is challenging for insecure leadership. Egos cannot win over a healthy culture. Therefore, for such leaders to develop healthy cultures can be threatening, since it can sometimes render a particular leader unnecessary. In my own case, I have become unnecessary to the health of BluEra, so that the organization could survive without me. To some, this is frightening, because they derive their meaning from their role and power position in the organization—a mindset validated by the leader.

In his book *Leaders Eat Last*, Simon Sinek argues that leaders should see their people as their children. While his overall message is outstanding, and I feel it's important to cultivate a love for the people who work with you, the power dynamic between parent and child isn't in my judgment ideal in the workplace. We are all our own boss. No one can own another person's experience. The relationship between the leader and the team, therefore, needs to be one that's more akin to twins, whereby there is parallel development and mutual respect.

Suppose your company has never really thought about its culture—never intentionally evolved a culture. Because corporate culture is malleable, it can be developed. Existing cultures can also be transformed. The engine of transformation is the ability to grow from lessons learned. For this reason, evolving an effective culture can be a great place to start on the task of awakening your company.

Zappos' Tony Hsieh came to see that the road to profitability involves creating a humane culture. He realized that, since personnel function best in a humane environment, a humane workplace motivates and engages them. Hsieh's belief that the best customer experience is a natural extension of a healthy culture has been validated. At Zappos, such a culture has resulted in providing top notch customer service. For this reason, instead of spending money on advertising and marketing, Zappos relies on satisfied customers and word of mouth to market them.[3]

Do you consciously consider each of your customers as a marketer for your company? When you give customers what they are looking for—not only in terms of product, but also in your manner of dealing with them—they are likely to become loyal promoters of your brand. When they tell their neck of the woods about you, word tends to spread at the grassroots. This can be far more powerful than advertising you can buy.

One can sometimes feel a company's energy, or lack

thereof, and its distinct personality upon entering its doors. For instance, have you ever set foot in a business and felt your energy sink—or, conversely, entered a business and been almost instantly energized? When corporate cultures emphasize profitability over quality relationships among their personnel, the results are not only unpleasant, but can seriously impact the success of the company.

Awakened companies know the value of a synthesis of diverse parts of the organization. They learn how to create and nurture connective tissue within the organization, using relationships to maintain good communication between the different departments or sections of the company. They also recognize there are ways to do this beyond just the accomplishment of tasks. For example, awakened companies recognize that playing and celebrating together builds rapport, which fosters cross-fertilization of ideas between related disciplines and teams.

This lightness is in no way a lack of seriousness, but is a matter of being at ease, since a lightness in a company is buoying and energizing. A fun atmosphere stimulates brainstorming because the individuals in the company feel less restrained and censored. Play is an important component of creativity. When the creative flow is supported by lightness, even the craziest ideas can get heard. In an atmosphere of playful exploration, the kind of ideas that create new frontiers—not only in business, but in the ways we live in the world—can come forth, ideas that aren't initially obvious. For example, it was once thought ridiculous that people would ever want a computer in their homes. Many "common sense" business people turned down the early innovators of the home computer. This is an obvious example, but there are many. Now, spray-on skin and driverless cars have moved from science fiction to reality, and flying cars may be about to follow.[4]

Awakened companies see the connection between positive playful creativity and success. Canadian W. Brett Wilson[5], former chairman of FirstEnergy and chairman and investor in Canoe Financial, as well as founder and owner of Prairie Merchant Corporation (PMC), says, "You know, every single person in my office has the word *fun* in their title. Robin's title is Manager of Brett Wrangling and Fun. There's a Manager of Office Operations and Fun. My technology guy is Vice President of Technology, Magic, and Fun." Wilson adds in jest, "The President doesn't have the word fun because we say he's no fun. He's got to run the business."

An intelligently structured environment should allow for lighthearted interaction without it devolving into constant unproductive clowning. An awakened executive knows the importance of people letting off steam and recognizes when a good laugh is called for. Such an executive also knows when to bring levity into really tough situations—and, conversely, when to honor heavy emotions and stress by allowing space for them.

People Work Here

Each awakening company culture will be different, depending on the kind of industry, the broader culture they are nested in, their corporate mission, and other factors. However, all of these companies will have one thing in common. They will all be humane work environments.

Beyond the quality of relationships in a company, other factors translate into a humane workplace, an important one of which is the work environment itself. The awakened company understands that if a culture is to support healthy interactions among personnel, it's helpful for this to be reflected in the look and feel of the team's surroundings. Does the office space foster cohesiveness, or are people separated based on perceived rank or division? And what are we saying to ourselves, our employees, and the wider community by stuffing people in identical, sanitized, fluorescent-lighted cubicles? Are we suggesting personnel are faceless cogs in a machine? What effect does this have on the cohesiveness and morale of the company, and is it cost-effective in the long run? In any organization, if we lose a sense of humanity, we are also losing the soul of the organization.

Recognizing the importance of supporting a humane culture, awakened companies place an emphasis on workplace aesthetics. This is why, in Canada for instance, Cirque du Soleil and some of the big fashion companies focus on aesthetics—something that's also increasingly true of companies in Silicon Valley in the United States. It shows a particular lack of vision when businesses don't allow the display of individual art or photos.

In contrast, awakened companies encourage individual expression in the workplace. They recognize the importance of valuing our humanness, which leads them to provide a work environment that encourages personal connection and invites individual expression. For instance, Zappos seeks to make their work environment not only humane and creative, but "festive." To foster this spirit, employees are encouraged to express their unique personalities. In a different way, Shawna Guiltner,[6] who is CEO of NGC Product Solutions in Canada and one of the rare female CEOs in Alberta's oil patch, ensures that not only is her team treated well, but the team's furry friends are also welcomed to their office. It's part of her belief that business needs to make the world a safer place, which is a key element of her vision for the company.

Smart companies understand that an appreciation for aesthetics has a tendency to extend to every aspect of the work itself. Beauty and elegance of design are reflected in the beauty and elegance with which personnel accomplish tasks. This can include everything from a team member who multitasks with a completely calm, graceful, and quiet demeanor, to a waiter who pours a glass of water with a flourish from a pitcher raised high above the customer's seated position.

Given that biodiversity is essential to our planet's survival, should we be surprised that diversity also helps human systems thrive? Instead of forcing everyone to fit into a mold, awakened companies are champions of diversity. They consider what living a beautiful life looks like and recognize that providing an inviting and supportive space for employees helps them feel appreciated. In such an atmosphere, people are more relaxed, which inspires creativity, innovation, and productivity.

It shows a particular lack of vision when executives have beautifully designed offices, yet this appreciation for aesthetics doesn't extend to the workers. The executive offices may be elegant, whereas the employees get ugly cubicles.

When executives with this mentality think outside the box or express their creativity on matters not directly related to a project, this is described as visionary and unorthodox brilliance. An employee who does the same is seen as wasting time, being disruptive, or making unreasonable demands for a better work environment. Often, the same executive who values his own creative "maverick" tendencies suppresses the same in employees. The final irony is that this kind of unawakened executive would refuse to serve as an employee in their own company under these conditions.

Not everyone has to have the same degree of aesthetic beauty in their work environment. However, everyone's workspace needs to reflect a spirit of collaboration, flexibility, and fairness.

Individuals Make a Culture

Craig Kielburger, of Me To We, describes their corporate culture as "idealistic." He adds, "In fact, I'd say shamelessly idealistic—and entrepreneurial. We define ourselves as social entrepreneurs."

This process begins with hiring practices. To this end, Kielburger explains, "We hire for culture first and foremost, more than for skill one might even say."

"When we hire staff," says Kolin Lymworth,[7] founder of Banyen books in Vancouver, BC, "it's not like we're just performing a task, or we're looking for someone who can do the task. We want people who identify with our mission. It means something to them, they want to be in this environment and do this kind of work."

Says Tony Hsieh, with reference to Zappos' hiring practices, "We've passed on a lot of really smart, talented people that we know can make an immediate impact on our top or bottom line. But if they're bad for our culture, we won't hire them for that reason alone."[8] Hsieh goes on to explain that even a superstar in terms of their job function will be let go if they are a detriment to the company culture.

Hiring is something of which, as a recruiter for companies,

I have considerable personal knowledge. As part of the recruiting process, I ask in the interview what their values are. In one interview, an individual responded that their personal name is their value. Thus when they stand behind a company, they must believe in it. This reflects a relaxed sense of integrity. Knowing what you stand for is key—a topic we will return to in due course.

According to a recent Harvard Business Review blog, it's important to hire for values, then shape a job for the person, versus shaping a job and hiring people for fit.[9]

Ensuring a company has sufficient diversity is also important when hiring. We all harbor a number of deeply held psychological biases, one of which is the "similar to me effect." From my experience, this is problematic. I've noticed that people normally choose to work with people who are like them, which doesn't always work. When coworkers have similar strengths and weaknesses, there's an overlap of talent and a deficit in many areas. I've also noticed that people working together who are too similar tend to get angry, frustrated, or withdraw more often than those with different strengths and weaknesses.

While it can help to have some initial chemistry between two people for them to want to further interact with one another, it's important to go beyond that initial "click" with candidates and people in your business, cultivating a deep awareness of who they are. What motivates them? What differences do you have with them?

A common trap is to dismiss someone because there's no obvious chemistry. Often there are hidden gems we can't pick up on in the first meeting, and we miss out if we don't investigate further. A potential connection needs time to breathe.

The more diverse a team is, the more profitable a company tends to be. As Ernst & Young's Groundbreakers Report in 2008 states, "Academic research has established that diverse groups of people tend to outperform homogeneous groups if both groups' members have equal abilities." The report adds, "We should do more than just exploit our current diversity; we may want to encourage even greater functional diversity, given its benefits."[10]

It goes without saying that fairness and inclusion go hand in hand with an enlightened and compassionate company. Diversity and gender balance can be found at all levels of the workforce. Both the male and female perspectives are present in the organization, and people of diverse cultures, social orientations, and skills are welcomed for their unique energy and perspectives.

Diversity means a greater collective ability, and therefore increased profitability. Balanced companies have an open, energetic, merging quality to them, where all colors of the rainbow can manifest and be expressed. A multitude of perspectives come out, and right action emerges as a result of seeing all these perspectives.

At the same time, it needs to be acknowledged that when so much diversity is actively encouraged, a diversity of opinions can lead to conflict. Healthy debate is to be encouraged, but always with compassion and respect for each individual. Employees are reminded of how important harmony is for our health and wellbeing, as well as for maintaining a dynamic flow and synergy in the company.

Page and Hong from Loyola University in Chicago discovered that "the collective ability of any crowd is equal to the average ability of its members, plus the diversity of the group."[11] These findings were so consistent that they created a mathematical theorem to express it, concluding that "the diversity of the group's members matters as much as their ability and brainpower, if not more." Increasing diversity should no longer be thought of as merely a feel-good mantra, but as Page says, "It's a mathematical fact."

4

A RETURN TO COMMUNITY

How would you like to work in a supportive company that's prosperous, energized, sustaining, and generative? I am referring to a company that doesn't adversely affect your mental, emotional, and physical health in the way many workplaces do, but that makes you feel safe and valued.

Welcome to the world of commerce of the future—a future that's unfolding even now in a growing number of businesses.

As we awaken to the importance of community, it becomes natural to spontaneously include more people in our sense of self, and therefore in our extended human family. This, along with a newfound desire to align our personal and business values, encourages a focus on creating a humane company culture.

Some large well-known organizations are already leading the pack in creating caring business communities. Whole Foods Market has a set of management principles that begin with love, while PepsiCo lists "caring" as its first guiding principle on its website. Zappos also explicitly focuses on caring as part of its values, stating, "We are more than a team. We are a family. We watch out for each other, care for each other, and go above and beyond for each other."[1]

The quality of the relationships in any company tends to define the corporate culture, and this is unique to each organization. The quality of specific relationships produces the interactions that bring a community to life. However, the influence goes both ways, in that the quality of the community affects the individuals and relationships, as well.

In other words, business relationships are reciprocal, in that the nature of a company influences the individuals and relationships within it, and vice versa. It's a dynamic system. Living beings constitute the company, synergies create and maintain the corporate entity, and the enterprise develops a life of its own that's beyond any one person or set of relationships.

Henry Mintzberg, Cleghorn Professor of Management Studies at McGill University, stresses the importance of regarding all personnel as human beings like ourselves. In line with this, he advocates redesigning the workplace to change the way business is done. "I think it's simply a question of stopping the mistreatment of people, and there are a number of things that could be done," he says. "The first thing is to get rid of the terms human resources, human assets, and human capital. I'm a human being, not a human asset, human resource, or human capital. Companies should be run as communities of human beings, not collections of human resources."

Mintzberg goes further: "The second thing they could do is stop firing people every time they don't make their stock market expectations. We need to rid ourselves of the idea that somehow 5,000 people suddenly need to be made redundant because the stock price has dropped and the CEO's bonus is threatened. Executive bonuses should be completely revamped. Any chief executive who accepts to be paid

300-400 times as much as the workers in the company isn't a leader. The message sent out is, 'I'm that many hundreds of times more important than anybody else.' That's no way to engage and encourage people in the company."

Since the only truly sustainable economy is an awakened economy, cultivating awareness is a key goal for MIT's Otto Scharmer, whose *Theory U* presumes that "the quality of results in any kind of socio-economic system is a function of the awareness that people in the system are operating from." Scharmer argues that if we are to save our planet, a highly aware society must produce the next economy. He refers to this economy as "compassion-based," following the principle that the more we give, the more we receive.

Becoming a self-aware human being is the foundation for success in any business. Companies with self-aware personnel who aspire to excellence are effective, efficient, and exhibit professionalism and class. Each team member's growing ability to observe themselves makes the company as a whole better at learning, spotting trends, keeping abreast of what's going on in their industry and community, and adapting to current situations.

When success is narrowly defined, companies can become obsessed with goals, which tends to result in a lack of compassion. This is the sweat shop mentality that, leaving a sense of humanity at the door, drives poor decisions. It's also reflected in the caffeinated, adrenalized workspace where we can't see the bigger picture. This driven competitiveness tends to cause people to stop communicating honestly. With little ability to come from an authentic inner place, the company image becomes dominant, often accompanied by a lack of star quality.

Awareness Leads to Caring and Sharing

Awakened executives know that care and service must extend to the wider community and the planet itself. In terms of compassion and service, when we draw the line at our company door, we draw a line around ourselves reflecting the limits of our self-awareness and awareness of our interdependence.

Businesses with a humane culture understand that high quality relationships within the organization automatically extend to their clients. As the Harvard Business Review pointed out more than a decade ago, "The service profit chain establishes relationships between profitability, customer loyalty, employee satisfaction, loyalty, and productivity. The links in the chain (which should be regarded as propositions) are as follows: Profits and growth are stimulated primarily by customer loyalty. Loyalty is a direct result of customer satisfaction. Satisfaction is largely influenced by the value of services provided to customers. Value is created by satisfied, loyal, and productive employees. Employee satisfaction, in turn, results primarily from high quality support services and policies that enable employees to deliver results to customers."[2]

Emphasizing the seismic nature of this different way of relating, Henry Mintzberg states, "It's a total shift in attitudes really. It's a shift not only involving people working for the company, but involving customers. It's about not exploiting people for every last cent. It means we don't bamboozle customers with pricing nobody can understand, and we don't exploit people because there are a few bucks to be made here and there. It's about customers who are valued. The same goes for suppliers, who need to be treated decently because it's not a question of squeezing money out of them for the next year or two, but of fostering sustainable relationships."

Weighing in on why making money can't be a business' chief raison d'être, the world-renowned teacher of the importance of relishing each moment of life, Eckhart Tolle—author of *The Power of Now* and *A New Earth*—explains, "An enlightened person or business is not concerned primarily with making money, because when you are concerned with making money you want the future more than the present. Whenever you want the future more than you want the present, true intelligence cannot flow into what you do, because it can do so only when you are totally aligned with the present moment. So, instead, what you do is ego, or it comes from ego."[3]

It's for this reason that Zappos call center representatives focus on the quality of their interactions with customers. Known as the Customer Loyalty Team, they understand that creating a *personal emotional connection* with the customer improves and humanizes the customer experience. Instead of pushing customers to get down to business, they might inquire how a customer's day is going or ask them about their holiday plans. Team members are counted upon to do whatever is necessary to satisfy customers. They are encouraged to send flowers, cookies, or coupons to select customers at their discretion. They are also given 15 minutes before lunch to write thank you cards to some of the customers with whom they have interacted. The success of this business model is reflected in the fact that three out of four of Zappos' customers are repeat business, and their sales have surpassed $2 billion.[4]

Matrix seeks to foster a spirit of giving, sharing, and helping among its employees. To actively encourage their personnel to help each other, the company designed an in-house mentorship program and training programs in which colleagues teach each other new skills. These programs, along with the frequent town halls that Rob Pockar,[5] CEO of Matrix, personally conducts at their offices in different cities, help embed the company culture in personnel. The company even created a Senior VP of Culture and Communications "to help propagate and explain and evolve and celebrate our culture."

A Global Family

Zappos takes their culture of caring beyond their personnel and clientele, extending it to other businesses. To share their relationship values with these businesses, in a sense giving away the secrets of their competitive advantage,[6] the Zappos Insights Program invites companies to come and learn how to create their own unique culture. Consequently, people from everywhere come to the Las Vegas headquarters to take a tour and learn about their unique culture.

Additionally, through the Zappos Insights Program, businesses and business leaders participate in boot camps to learn how to "empower and engage employees to excel, and wow customers."[7] So committed is the company to a dynamic culture, that their operational independence remained non-negotiable even after the company was purchased by Amazon in 2009.[8]

Another company openly sharing its expertise is SELCO Solar. Says Dr. Hande, the company's philosophy is that "we are all in this together." By imparting their skills and knowledge to other companies and entrepreneurs, these potential rivals learn what works and what doesn't. Working to upgrade India's social enterprise structure by helping other entrepreneurs use his business model, Dr. Hande shows us that market-driven solutions can be cooperative instead of purely competitive. He believes that India has "a wonderful opportunity to show the world the right way of doing business."[9]

The *quality* of the help we give matters. In a typical cutthroat business environment, the success we enable in others will be limited and possibly short-lived if we aren't truly generous. If we are simply trying to generate as much profit for ourselves as possible, then the seeds for a prosperous community aren't being planted. Instead, we promote race-to-the-bottom lower quality service and inadequate wages, neither of which support a community's social and economic fabric.

Declaring that the spin-off from our existence in a community is help enough, while everyone is straining just to make ends meet, doesn't constitute success. If you have a garden and do the absolute minimum to keep its stunted plants barely alive, you don't label this success. Stretching employees, suppliers, and the community to the breaking point doesn't constitute a successful business.

To the degree we are more awake, we tend to notice the unity of things as a normal and natural perception. We don't find ourselves drawing imaginary lines around everything, naming and labeling as we pigeonhole people.

This approach of sharing with one another makes sense from a biological point of view. Now that we have been able to trace our DNA as a species, we realize that every human on the planet originated from a common mother in Africa. Like it or not, we are all members of a single family. Recognizing this, we can reframe competition in terms of our unity, which is what's happening with those companies that are assisting their competitors.

I can well imagine a CEO saying, "I certainly don't want to feel unity with my competitors." Entirely in the shadow in such a statement is the fact that the competition *is* the connection. Once we realize that we can't avoid being connected, we open the door to finding things we have in common with our competitors. Instead of causing us to go to war with one another, we begin to build on our similarities. The potential for hostility is replaced by the desire to spur one another on, which encourages both parties to develop themselves more fully.

Why Ego Gravitates to Doing Battle in Business

Ego is incapable of perceiving life's fundamental sacredness and connectedness because it develops from a disconnection from our deeper nature. This limited and distorted sense of "me" simply doesn't see the greater reality. The egoic filter causes us to perceive threats everywhere, which leads to the belief we need to be at war with other individuals, companies, or nations. Instead of seeing them as unique expressions of the infinite variety that naturally springs from the creative source of everything that exists, we regard them as competitors to be beaten.

The ego imagines that if, instead of warring with one another as we so frequently do in the business world, we were to share with one another, we would end up giving more than we receive. However, when we shift out of the hostile projections of ego and simply address situations as they are, we become aware of an underlying unity behind our diversity. This sense of connectedness alters our goals as individuals, communities, corporations, governments, and nations. We switch from seeing the other as an enemy we must prove to be better than or defeat, to wanting to share our insights and thereby help make one another prosperous.

Awakened companies celebrate both independence and interdependence. The supportive culture that encourages each member to be their very best as a worker and a human being carries over into the marketplace and society as a whole. These companies are unafraid of the competition. They can even celebrate the success of a competitor and learn from that success. The complete honesty that pervades such companies makes it easy to see and accept what others are doing better than themselves. They recognize there's room for many competitors, and that in fact a variety of businesses are required for a healthy community to sustain all of us.

In terms of the threat to ego, situations that cause us to feel exposed are invitations to explore something in ourselves. Suppose we discover we're afraid our idea will be copied or credited to someone else. Does it really matter? What about ourselves are we protecting? And what would it feel like were we to simply allow the situation to be as it is?

We are all connected, and by supporting one business, we support all the other businesses it supports. For example, if we support our local farmers market, all the businesses associated with the market benefit from it. Aiding others multiplies business success, creating a feedback loop that ripples through the community.

The competitive spirit can be said to have promoted innovation. However, in some ways it has also done the opposite. If you see the pie as limited, there's a tendency to come from a mindset of scarcity. Companies then battle with each other, putting one another down and practicing one-upmanship. In contrast, if you realize that the pie is unlimited, then one innovation becomes but a steppingstone to another. Instead of fighting over the same turf, you grow more turf. The mindset of scarcity is replaced by a sense of abundance in which we realize we've only begun to tap our ingenuity, opportunity is unlimited, and there's plenty for everyone. From this perspective, a cooperation-based mindset has the potential to take us much further, much faster than a competitive mindset in which a great deal of creative energy is wasted on worrying about what others are doing.

In other words, as we work together instead of against each other, paradoxically we become aware that life has an uncanny way of looking out for us, as a vast collective intelligence beyond our individual sense of identity emerges to inform our understanding and help us make optimal decisions.

Otto Scharmer sees this, which is why he refers to compassion-based economics as "Economics 4.0." The essence of this is that "the more I give, the more I get. So when I help others, it's in itself a source of wellbeing for me. And that's really what's needed."

Not only does a culture of caring produce great customer loyalty and cooperation between competitors, but it prevents negative and disruptive behavior on the part of businesses we have dealings with from infecting our company.

Recognizing how important it is to ensure that those businesses with unhealthy cultures don't infect our own, Northland's Ransdell comments, "We have a corporate value that's pretty basic, which is, 'Let's do business with people who like to do business with us, people who treat us how we want to be treated. Let's deal with businesses who respect us because they respect themselves. When you find a company that's like-minded, it's a nice fit. The pieces of the puzzle match up."

In addition, Northland's CEO Orn Gudmundsson adds, "We just have a nice atmosphere here, and it's my job to protect it and my job to staff, and culture's all about the people that you hire and how they treat one another and their level of self-esteem."[10]

5

AWAKENED LEADERSHIP

Have you ever been in the presence of someone you felt lifted up by, buoyed by? Someone who inspired you to want to improve your behavior? Awakened executives elevate the personnel within a company so that they contribute their highest attributes.

Comments Dr. Julian Barling,[1] Borden Professor of Leadership at Queen's School of Business, "Part of leadership is about creating a context in which others can excel."

Awakened executives invite others in the company to awaken to their interrelatedness with their fellow workers, the community in which the company functions, the wider environment of the planet, and of course their personal potential. As more and more individuals respond, together they impact the company's vision and culture. Functioning as an awakened team, they create a deeply satisfying environment that ultimately leads to greater corporate wellbeing and financial profitability.

Often, though not always, it's the executives who awaken first. They then help the employees and the company as a whole to awaken. Although anyone can activate this process within a company, perhaps even forming a pilot team of individuals focused on awakening, preferably it's the executives who initiate the process of transformation because of the rapid and profound impact such individuals can have on a company. As Tony Schwartz points out, "The energy of leaders is, for better or worse, contagious."[2]

The awakening executive realizes that their own continued growth requires awareness of the centrality of personal relationships. The awakening leader also realizes that a healthy culture isn't possible without healthy, awakening relationships. Since profitability and sustainability depend more than ever on a humane, healthy culture, what emerges is awareness of a direct correlation between healthy relationships and profits.

In contrast to the inspiration brought by awakened executives, we have all known leaders who fill the room with their own voice and have no real insight into their impact on others. Such egotists lead in a way in which the other isn't included. Not only do these leaders not value the opinions of others, but some even indulge in verbal lashings, snatch power and responsibility from others, take credit for the efforts of others, or are excessively results-driven. Constance Kellough, founder and president of Namaste Publishing, thinks that to take credit for another's effort, or withhold giving credit to another when due, is a form of theft.

In these and other ways, the unawakened executive creates a sense of being separate and isolated, which results in employee insecurity, distrust, and ultimately apathy. Incapable of perceiving the deeper truth of our interconnectedness and interdependence, such executives major in "us versus them," "win versus lose," and "fear versus caring."

Rose Marcario,[3] President and CEO of Patagonia, relates how the need for a different model of leadership became a reality in her own life. "I grew up in a model where leadership meant hierarchy and power over people," she recalls. "It majored in control, and one of its key features involved sectioning people off into specialties. I don't think that's healthy. We are whole human beings, which means there are many ways in which we can grow and work together. We don't thrive when we are shoehorned into a particular title or role. There needs to be flexibility, so that people not only have room to grow in their present niche but also have the opportunity to develop aspects of themselves they haven't so far been aware of."

For Marcario this comes down to a simple truth articulated by Dr. Hande, who explains, "It's about how you treat people, being kind even in a situation where someone has got to you."

Echoes Marcario, "I think that kindness is really at the heart of leadership," adding, "and I don't think that it's a weak kind of leadership."

Matrix's Rob Pockar agrees with this and asserts, "If you treat people like a peer, even if you're the CEO and they're the receptionist, it resonates through the organization that it is a human place. We talk about having a very flat organization. It's a community of colleagues." Regardless of someone's role, they are considered a peer. As Pockar puts it, "One of the things that we're trying to do is build a great community."

Echoing this, Otto Scharmer points to the fact that employees who feel they work in a loving, caring culture report higher levels of satisfaction and teamwork. Consequently, they show up to work more often.[4]

The Importance of One-on-One

ARC Financial's Van Wielingen believes that although we tend to think of a culture as "a big amorphous thing," relating it to "large groups and systems, and processes and big group meetings, and all the communication of a larger group," in reality a culture is "about the way we treat each other—and most profoundly, one-on-one."

Van Wielingen states plainly, "I think that the one-on-one experience creates culture." Explaining that the creative engine of a culture is to be found in "the way we treat each other in a current moment," he emphasizes that it's the meaningfulness of our one-on-one relationships that really makes the difference in a company's culture.

Why is one-on-one so important? "You know, when you're one-on-one, there's the immediacy of contact, and there is interaction, engagement, and there is closeness," says Van Wielingen. "You can read where the other person is because there's much more feedback in the immediate sense. Whereas when you're in a group, you may be sharing yourself, but you're looking around the room. You don't have, and really can't have, the same feeling as to where people are."

Van Wielingen brings the company culture down to a truly personal level, using a word he says he doesn't remember using in business "because it has a narrower connotation in our society." The word to which he's referring is "intimacy," which he defines as a "palpable sense of contact with another person, whereby you share yourself in a direct way."

Clarifying how this works in actual corporate practice, Van Wielingen explains, "I don't mean hearing my secrets; I just mean, 'Here's my experience. This is how I'm viewing this. These are my concerns. What do you think?' There's a real opportunity when you are managing people to really give your attention to the other—to really confer, really let the other know that you see them, and that you can see their uniqueness as a human, not just as somebody who is filling a role in the organization."

Scharmer tells us, "People who worked in a culture where they felt free to express affection, tenderness, caring, and compassion for one another were more satisfied with their jobs, committed to the organization, and accountable for their performance."[5]

Personnel Who Are Personally Involved

Integrating our business life and our personal life makes sense because, as Joel Solomon,[6] chairman of Renewal Funds, which invests in change by providing an opportunity for investors to participate in the development of businesses at the forefront of social and environmental innovation, puts it, "The workplace is obviously where many of us spend the most amount of our time. Since it's where we are most of the time when we are physically awake, it's prime time. It's therefore the home of much of what we experience about relationship, about purpose, about conscious behavior. We are engaged with people, and we're dealing with challenges, distractions, issues of efficiency, and all kinds of pressure." Hence the workplace is a logical place for practicing all aspects of life, "and therefore for making ourselves a more awakened person."

Patagonia is an example of a corporate culture that functions more like a family. Says Rose Marcario, CEO of Patagonia, "We have yoga classes a few times a week, which is nice, and other exercise classes, which I think promotes the sense that overall Patagonia is a very healthy environment and lifestyle." She adds, "We really promote and want our employees to take that time to take care of themselves."

Marcario's rationale for their family atmosphere has everything to do with business. As she puts it, "I think the best organizations try and help people move through whatever fear they have and become their most fully realized, engaged self. In my opinion, that company will win."

Patagonia also has "a communal café, so we have ways that we can connect with and see our friends and colleagues that we might not meet with in a meeting, or connect with in a meeting. It's just a nice, informal way to sort of have what I consider a communalist family kind of experience."

Another important factor in the feeling of being a family is Patagonia's daycare center, which Marcario describes as "all around here, and so the kids are everywhere. It's a terrific thing that parents have their children close and can be with them when they need to be with them and have lunch with them and just have that kind of experience."

Creating a Caring Community

Awakened leaders want employees to work together as human beings. To achieve this, they must ensure the interpersonal dynamics in a team are sound. One way to foster sound interpersonal dynamics is to engage in effective check-ins.

If a company is truly to function as a community, checking in with each other needs to be a frequent practice. However, at such times, it's important we go deeper than the current situation and its challenges. We must get to the level that we remove our employee masks for a time, allowing each other to see the real person behind our roles. This is what leads to the kind of caring that makes for real community.

At BluEra, we check in at the start of every week. People share where they are, what's going on in their lives, what's going well, and what sucks. Initially, for some this is uncomfortable, since they aren't used to bringing their whole self to the office and tend to talk only about work matters or what happened on their weekends. In due course, they realize that when they come to work, they come as a whole person, not just as a role.

In our check-in, we don't focus on the negative, even though we invite its expression. To ensure we avoid a focus on negativity, we sometimes allocate time to express appreciation. Every member of our team states what they appreciate about each person, or what they appreciate about the company they are working with. To close, we invite comments on what they learned from the meeting that just occurred. What went well and what didn't go well? This is non-personal and focused on the issues at hand.

During a check-in, it may emerge that there's conflict between two groups or two individuals. In such situations, the executive's involvement needs to go beyond seeking harmony. An awakened approach doesn't entail merely quieting things down so people can get on with a project, but requires healing conflict at its root. If the workplace is to be a truly caring environment, this is crucial.

To illustrate what it means to heal a conflict at its root, one of the members of an executive team kept on insisting that the team had real issues. When the majority didn't feel the same way as this particular team member, it became apparent that the energy he was projecting onto the team was an extension of what he was experiencing in his personal life. It turned out he was going through a really nasty divorce, involving a great deal of acrimony.

It's because employees' personal lives are so interwoven with their performance on the job, that Dr. Hande shows great concern when his colleagues are struggling with something of a personal nature. "We tell them the telephones are never off, so in the sense that you have a problem at 1 a.m., if it's a business related problem, then don't call," he explains. "But if it's a personal problem, call us 24/7. Business can always wait—we'll handle it tomorrow. So don't worry about it, and sleep well. If you have an issue that you think you need advice on, and it's something that's critical and hurting you, then call at 1 a.m., 1:30, or 2. It doesn't matter what time it is."

There's also evident concern for each other's personal issues and personal growth at Namaste Publishing. "We share so much on a personal level, all of us," president and publisher Constance Kellough confides. "I'm always here to talk to my colleagues about their personal issues, and they for me. We're so authentic with each other, transparent with each other. I mean, it's shoulder to shoulder. I care for them by showing how grateful I am all the time. The gratitude flows back and forth."

Kellough sums her approach up in a nutshell: "Every encounter should be a sacred one, whether it's with yourself, a customer, or a co-worker."

Eknath Easwaran, a spiritual teacher who was influenced by Mahatma Gandhi, once pointed out that when we respond to the joys and sorrows of others as if they were our own, we have "attained the highest state of spiritual union."

Having said this, leaders need to be balanced when it comes to personal issues. Such issues can creep into business in a way that undermines both the supportive atmosphere and the efficient functioning of the company. This will tend to hinder a company's mission, since a poisonous atmosphere can arise that goes from blaming and resentment to undermining and sabotaging. If a company were to allow this for too long, they would struggle to stay in business.

In caring, we don't want to become lost in another's state of being. It's a matter of catching ourselves in a lack of concern for the other as well as avoiding becoming enmeshed in their issues. Note that what appears as "too much caring" is actually getting lost in our thoughts about others, getting lost in the affairs of others. It's possible to listen deeply to another without reacting by going to either extreme, and this is the most helpful response we can make.

In addition to getting caught up in the drama of interpersonal dynamics, overvaluing personal issues can also lead to coddling. When a leader over-invests in people's problems, employees aren't being empowered to solve these problems themselves. A kind of co-dependency develops, not only blurring the boundaries in a company in an unhealthy way, but undercutting the individual's need to grow in self-awareness and the ability to manage their life responsibly. At issue is the difference between an open, caring heart, and one that absorbs everyone's issues and is full of hurt. The latter encourages individuals to take everything personally, attaching themselves to the drama of people's stories. When this happens, we mistake this for healthy compassion and concern. The key to being truly empathic is listening to our own inner being. We must know when to be hands on, but also when to be hands off.

When companies awaken to the reality that employees are part of their extended family, they realize that the slogan "business is business" is a horrible distortion of what work is really about. Business is far from just "business." It's deeply interwoven with the whole of life.

6

THE LAYERS WITHIN

Although a community comprises specific relationships and interactions that produce a synergy greater than the sum of its parts, it still relies heavily on its most fundamental component, the individual.

The CEO of American Express has been quoted as saying, "People are the company's greatest strength." For this reason, the individual's growing self-awareness is an important aspect of the wellbeing of a business community.

Whether we are aware of it or not, we are all in the process of developing our individual self-awareness. As slow or imperceptible as it may be, as we go through life, we are constantly expanding our sense of who we are. Even when we behave in a way that reflects lessened self-awareness, we are presented with an opportunity to learn from this experience—as can those around us.

An awakened company is one in which personnel at every level develop the ability to observe whatever may be happening in a given work situation with an attitude of healthy "curiosity, openness, and acceptance."[1] When there's curiosity, openness, and acceptance, creativity thrives.

Business Involves Learning About Ourselves

"Curiosity, openness, and acceptance" need to take two forms, one external and the other internal. On the one hand we open ourselves up to seriously consider all the options placed before us, as discussed in earlier chapters, while on the other we quietly observe any impulses that arise within us—observe without acting on these impulses. This is different than thinking about what we are doing. We are simply noticing.

The purpose of observing ourselves is to develop the ability to *pause* before we act.[2] Simply by developing the capacity to pause instead of reacting, we give ourselves an opportunity to rework who we understand ourselves to be. Our whole sense of ourselves may then begin to change, and this can open up new horizons for both ourselves and others.

The ability to pause—to exercise flexibility in how and when we respond to a situation—allows us to bypass our impulses, providing us with a way to be our "wisest self possible in that moment."[3] Simply experiencing our situation as it *is* right now becomes far more important and informative than the stream of thoughts and emotions that tend to dominate our awareness at any given moment. We find ourselves paying attention to what's *actually happening,* not to what we think about the situation or fantasize concerning it.

Hence a key aspect of an awakening organization is that it has a high percentage of individuals who are increasingly responsible for their actions—not least of which are their reactions. They are people who are developing a strong combination of self-control and self-discipline. Only when the authentic teamwork that springs from such a capacity for responsibility reaches a tipping point, becoming our dominant modus operandi, are we equipped to effectively address the inevitable challenges that arise whenever people work together.

This reworking of our self-understanding in turn alters our understanding of others, along with our interpretation of situations. As the illusion that we are some small, isolated piece of an indifferent universe falls away, we find ourselves more willing to let go of our entrenched positions, our tired self-concepts, our limited thinking.

How to Establish an Inquiring Atmosphere in Your Business

Google is famous for offering "mindfulness" courses to its employees. You may have heard this word in other contexts, and people can mean different things when they use it. So, when a company like Google refers to mindfulness, what exactly do they have in mind?

As a blog explains, "Mindfulness is, quite simply, the skill of being present and aware, moment by moment, regardless of circumstances."[4] In other words, mindfulness is what we've been seeing concerning the need to address situations as they really are and not as they may appear through the projections of our self-image.

Mindfulness is sometimes confused with a mood or a particular state of mind, whereas it would be more accurate to say that it's the ability to pay greater attention—to be aware of whatever mood or state of mind we might be in. As mentioned earlier, this isn't the same as thinking about such things. It's more fundamental to our human experience than this. For example, we can be aware we are thinking. This is quite different from thinking about thinking. Most of us can tell when we or others are more awake and "with it," contrasted with those times when our attention is preoccupied or dispersed. In terms of business, how can we do our best work if our attention isn't fully on what we are doing?

Says management guru Bill George, "In my experience, mindful people make better leaders than frenetic ones." Why might this be? The answer may lie in a phenomenon we encountered earlier—neuroplasticity. As it turns out, "Researchers have found that mindfulness can reprogram the brain to be more rational and less emotional."[5]

George spells out the effects of this finding: "They understand their reactions to stress and crises, and understand their impact on others. They are far better at inspiring people to take on greater responsibilities and at aligning them around common missions and values."

Earlier, we talked about hiring practices. Now we can add the importance of hiring for self-awareness. In line with George's insight, Erik Kaae,[6] former SMS&P director for Denmark and Iceland at Microsoft and now COO of EG, Denmark's largest supplier of practitioner IT systems, comments, "When I am selecting new leaders, I always spend a lot of time asking questions like how well do they actually understand themselves. Because if you don't understand yourself and you don't understand your weaknesses, how can you help other people? That's sort of my key belief. Those who do not recognize themselves for the whole person they are, I suggest courses for them."

In addition to sending their personnel on courses, some companies hire personal coaches to help with team members' development. For example, Zappos has an in-house life coach for all its employees. They find they function more effectively not only when team members understand the company's values, but when they are also cognizant of their own strengths and weaknesses.

What Self-observation Can Show Us

As we become more skillful in our self-observation, we will see many wonderful things about ourselves that we either hadn't noticed before or haven't really taken in. Successful transformation requires us to affirm and nurture those characteristics that are our assets. Recognizing our gifts empowers us to act confidently when required.

Even as we uncover the ways in which each of us is capable of gracing life with our unique expressions of creativity, under the scrutiny of genuine self-observation, we are bound to encounter elements of our personality—along with elements of the ethics, values, and structures of our business world—that constitute a shadow side of our creativity and can be difficult to face up to.

It's nearly impossible to engage in real development without becoming aware of those elements of our makeup that, without our realizing it, have been holding us back not only personally, but also as businesses, a species, and a planet. As awareness of our interior world increases, and we notice patterns to our thinking, emoting, and behavior, we will likely discover that it isn't always pleasant to see the ways we react to things. Such reactions can be difficult to acknowledge, let alone fully own.

Nevertheless, awakening to the fact we are a powerful person with something truly worthwhile to contribute during our time to walk the earth necessitates becoming aware of our unconscious habits, both in our work patterns and in our personal life. These may run the gamut from being lost in thought much of the time, to acting impulsively, eating for emotional reasons instead of when we're truly hungry, or drinking to excess in order to numb ourselves to the unpleasant realization we are trapped in a situation that's either boring or painful.

In short, becoming self-aware is becoming aware of all of the different parts of ourselves, some of which will seem more familiar, and some of which may surprise us. The good news is that as we come to know our strengths, and to feel more confident in those strengths, the challenging parts of our personalities feel less threatening. We are able to address our more problematic issues using our intelligence, along with less defensiveness or self-judgment. This becomes a powerful and practical asset.

Most of us are far more defensive and unaware of our tendency to self-sabotage than we realize. Conducting an autopsy on our behavior, we may see a tendency to be negative, to refute, to block, to shut down a line of inquiry without due process. Conversely, we may discover we have a habit of jumping on a hobby horse without thorough research, thereby making poorly thought out decisions that we then bulldoze through—all the more so when there's the momentum of a consensus. These are the kinds of tendencies that can't be ignored and must be confronted, no matter how painful. A lack of self-awareness and of skillfully working with these personal tendencies can sink a company.

It's because the process of awakening to our potential is simultaneously exhilarating and challenging, that it requires courage. Such courage is spurred on as we spontaneously find ourselves experiencing a steady decline in our customary unease, a reduction of our pervasive anxiety, and a lessening of our dissatisfaction. Such progress in the quality of our day furnishes the motivation to continue the journey of awakening.

Ego and Truth

It may be shocking to some, but most of us have cherished ideas about ourselves that aren't exactly the truth. We may believe we have abilities or have established habits we don't really possess, or we may think we are free of difficulties others can plainly see are still present. Sometimes we may think we are actually worse than we really are, not seeing the good in ourselves or recognizing our gifts. Needless to say, we often hold similarly distorted views of others, especially people who are important to us.

For this reason, real change requires letting go of some of our cherished opinions. For example, one of my beliefs was that to be strong, I needed to be in control. If our personnel were feeling overwhelmed, I took control of the situation. The wiser course would have been to allow them to experience—and even stew in—the discomfort of their feelings until they themselves either devised a solution or were motivated to seek my help in creating a solution.

As we seek self-understanding, it's helpful to avoid looking first to the mind, which tends to analyze. Far preferable is that we give our full attention to our body. Self-inquiry needs to be a *felt* experience, not an intellectual exercise. It needs to involve the gut, representing the entire body, along with the heart and the head. This full engagement with ourselves allows a deeper "knowing" to arise. This experiential awareness is naturally put into thoughts and words afterwards.

Our ego not only makes us feel separate from each other,

but from pretty much everything, essentially compartmentalizing reality. It's this state that enables people to believe that businesses, or any kind of structure for that matter, can operate in isolation. Business is business, family is family, community is community, the environment is the environment, and "never the twain shall meet." Such is the egoic distortion of reality.

It's a matter of not allowing our ego to get in the way. When we make an identity out of the constant stream of thoughts in our head, coupled with our emotional reactions, "me and my story" gets superimposed on our awareness of what's actually transpiring at any given moment. This personal sense of identity often resists the reality of the situation, which explains how we make what later come to be acknowledged as mistakes. Many of our mistakes are simply a case of misapplying old ideas—the ones we are in the habit of supplying—to situations that require a new and more creative response.

This isn't to say that our personal sense of self doesn't have a role to play. For example, being aware that we are separate individuals keeps our body safe in the physical environment, while allowing us to engage in the practicalities of social interaction. In the context of the personal self, many thoughts and emotions arise related to our wellbeing, some of which are appropriate and some of which are fantastical. We also have habits and learned routines that can be useful. It's just that such habits work well as tools, and much less so as the managers of our affairs. Mindfulness, coupled with self-awareness, allow us to discriminate in terms of which are the most useful.

A problem occurs when we become identified with those particular patterns of thought and emotion that don't tally with reality. The more we identify with these patterns, the less aware we become of what's actually happening. If we continue down this path, our thoughts and emotions may become compulsive, leading to paranoid and ruthless behavior like that of J. Edgar Hoover and Joe McCarthy. We then perceive reality through a heavily biased conceptual filter, which we are unable to switch off. Incapable of sensing the sacredness of life, we lose touch with compassion and become closed to the wisdom, creative genius, and goodwill of our fellow humans. Oblivious of our collective oneness, we incite division—and the squabbling that accompanies it reigns in place of the unity of working together as a team, thereby undercutting our human potential, if not torpedoing it.

What's Really Happening When We Find Ourselves Squabbling

Because relationships are so critical in business, we need to find ways to make them predominantly harmonious, otherwise we won't work together effectively. Having said this, human relationships inevitably face moments of tension and misunderstanding. Although the emphasis in the world of business is on practicality, our work is no different from our private life in this respect.

Since places of business can be arenas for disdain, anger, envy, and backstabbing, it's important to recognize that when such behavior causes us grief, it isn't really about others. Rather, it concerns the way we feel about *ourselves*. What we react to almost always gets to us because it's touching on something in ourselves we either haven't yet become aware of or haven't dealt with sufficiently.

It's easy to see this if, when we feel upset with another person, we ask who is feeling this. The answer, of course, is that *we* are, not the other person. In fact, we may have no clue what the other is feeling. However, whenever we react to being put down or to hostility, we are for sure feeling it. For this reason, if we can't engage the other in a healthy way for their sake, we must do so for our own sake.

Giving each other space in a relationship isn't a function of someone being either near or far from us in terms of our connection, but of inhabiting *ourselves* in each and every moment. Whether we are actually interacting with a colleague or just thinking about them, we are in relationship with them. Even if we withdraw from them due to anger or frustration, this psychological and emotional rejection is still a condition of attachment to the other, since fending them off only *appears* to protect our space.

That the real issue isn't the other's behavior, atrocious though it may be, but what it's triggering in us, can be seen from the way our body reacts in such situations. In discussing who we are and how we relate, heart and mind tend to take top billing, with our body an afterthought, if it's mentioned at all. However, the body reveals our true feelings and current level of awareness. Whether the body is tense or relaxed is a barometer of how awake we are.

Quite apart from the way we tense up when there's tension between ourselves and another, many of us feel unease in our body on a daily basis, as if we were reacting to a physical threat that doesn't actually exist. A clenched jaw, a tight abdomen, a constricted throat, and tense muscles indicate we are reacting to our *thoughts* about a situation, not necessarily to what's actually happening. We are essentially saying "no" to the present moment, unable to accept the here and now as it is. Working directly with such tensions is a powerful way to disengage from the defensive patterns of our ego.

The cluttered mind and the tight body of someone who is in a state of resistance leads not only to closed-mindedness, but to a closed heart and closed body language. Particularly if we are upset, we may actually feel the area around our heart tighten or close up. In a state of either avoidance or resistance, our arms may be crossed, our head tilted back, and our feet pointed away from whoever is in front of us.

When we feel upset about something or someone, whether a project or colleague, it's valuable to explore what exactly it is that's upsetting us. What about it is niggling at us? Where do we feel it, and can we trace its roots? This isn't merely a mental exercise. We can actually locate where these thoughts and emotions are registering in our body.

It simply doesn't occur to most of us that the reason we feel crowded, pressured, or upset by another has to do with our own state. However, if our buttons are getting pressed, we need to remind ourselves they are *our* buttons—our personal issues that were there long before the current upset. We should also keep in mind that it takes a lot of energy to defend against and ignore others, and it's this huge drain on our energy that causes us to feel crunched and cramped. To be lost in thought and emotional reactivity, as many of us are, is to live life under pressure. Often it isn't life and its requirements that drain us, even though we imagine this to be the case. Rather, it's our enormous and mostly unconscious resistance to things, which manifests in our body as tension.

As we become more grounded in our body, an unexpected thing happens. The inner noise in our head—our incessant inner chatter—becomes much quieter. This is the opposite of some kind of spaced-out trance. We actually can think more clearly.

Genuine relatedness is much more likely when the voice in the head that pretends to be each of us falls silent. No longer lost in what's often meaningless conversation with ourselves, we are free to give our full attention to a colleague, which allows them to feel our presence. As we interact with others from relaxed, grounded, clear-headed awareness, others feel less encroached upon.

To encounter real presence creates a feeling of space in place of the pressure the other person might be experiencing. The individual no longer suffers the duress of feeling crowded. Despite the problems that may have emerged, there's no urge to disengage or perhaps even abandon the relationship altogether. The groundedness of an awakened person means it doesn't matter whether we are alone or interacting with people, since others have ceased to be a burden or major irritation.

Separateness within Oneness

Working relationships often have a feel-good honeymoon phase during which there is evident caring. Then, as we get to know one another, we tend to start noticing what's not so "right" with each other. As Ginger Lapid-Bogda, an internationally recognized Enneagram author, trainer, keynote speaker, and coach, states, "pinches" or little annoyances begin occurring.

For example, one party always shows up late or doesn't respond to emails. A colleague regularly interrupts you. Someone else tries to push relationship boundaries. Another throws temper tantrums in the office. Each person's little faults and patterns now loom large, often eclipsing the qualities that drew us to them. The honeymoon comes to an end.

Most often pinches start small, then increase in their annoyance and even accumulate, which can lead to a blowup. When this happens, the person may leave the company. However, an alternative is to use such a blowup as an opportunity for a more real and honest relationship to emerge. The situation is an opportunity for people to gain an understanding of what the expectations are in the relationship. When expectations are better understood, the relationship will still have its ups and downs, but the baseline is clear.

If time produces a toxic effect, turning small things into mountains, the relationship isn't awakened. Instead, we have immersed ourselves in our historic opinions and fears, driven by wants and false expectations. The vast and pervasive sacredness of people has been lost from view. Consequently, there's a paucity of new wisdom and insight with respect to each other and the projects we are working on.

The hallmark of an awakened relationship is that we are separate individuals who recognize there's ultimately no separation. Acknowledging our interconnectedness informs our thinking about the best way to proceed with any projects we do together.

Healthy relationships in the workplace are not only possible, but I would argue they are inevitable once we are awake. Because to be awake is to operate in the here and now, we move beyond our historic opinions of each other, which are often no more than our ego's take on the other, and see one another with fresh eyes.

People may not always want to work together, but they can accept that they are nevertheless dependent on each other for success and satisfaction. Emotional non-attachment is a powerful antidote to acrimony in relationships because it enables us to accept, which involves sitting quietly with whatever form of acrimony or annoyance may be occurring, instead of bouncing off the walls. Acceptance doesn't mean we necessarily like what's happening, but we are able to be open to how something is working out, with a minimum of reactivity.

Non-attachment creates a spaciousness within us that allows us to respond in the most appropriate way. Instead of a situation triggering our fears, we allow it to foster a greater openness, so that we see beyond what appears like an impasse to the potential it holds. In place of the impulse to react, which is an attempt to force our will onto a situation, we look for the possibilities the situation contains.

Non-attachment Turns Acceptance into a Springboard

When we practice non-attachment in a situation, in that we are no longer emotionally reactive, the acceptance that arises allows us to use the situation as a springboard by responding intelligently, creatively, and in a manner that furthers connection instead of destroying it. Non-attachment has an element of deep acceptance in it, allowing us to work with the reality of the situation, and thus, freeing up our creative energy.

Many tend to confuse acceptance with acquiescence, but the two have nothing in common. Indeed, we need to realize that it's only when we accept the reality being presented to us that we are able to act wisely within the situation. The key is to notice whatever it is we have a resistance to, then—instead of fighting it—identify what we can and can't control. By allowing what's arising, we open up the flow of potential. Resistance serves only to dam the flow.

When we find it difficult to respond to provocation or a difficult situation with acceptance, it can be helpful to adopt the Buddhist practice called Tonglen, in which we breathe in another's pain and breathe out the energy we wish for that person. You might want to try this when a team member behaves in a way that causes you to react to them. Instead of feeling hostile to the individual, you'll find yourself feeling compassion for them.

It's an axiom that whenever we go deep enough into our oneness, the feeling that arises is that of caring—and as we have been seeing, caring on every level is at the core of a truly sustainable business, since there's a direct connection between our awareness of the sacredness of relationships and the bottom line.

I again want to point out that compassion, and the caring it results in, doesn't involve coddling. Rather, compassion aligns our intelligence with our heart so that we respond in a helpful way.

Even as compassion for someone doesn't mean coddling them, neither does being compassionate toward ourselves mean treating ourselves with kid gloves. On the contrary, sometimes it's more about facing difficult truths than about cheering ourselves up. It takes compassion to look honestly at the ways we aren't in alignment with reality, but only to the degree that we self-confront do we truly care for ourselves. To take our humanity to task requires courage and willpower.

Self-caring is an important antidote to burnout. Part of being honest with ourselves involves being able to discriminate between those times when it's essential to "go for broke," and when it's necessary to renew and restore. If, instead of using ourselves well, we abuse ourselves, this will be reflected in the kind of reactivity that's abusive of others. When such reactivity is rife in a company, it has a way of replicating itself in larger settings, showing up in such trends as depletion of the resources of our organization.

One reason companies benefit from encouraging their employees to become more self-aware is that, when a company has a growing number of awakened individuals who—rather than coming from ego, narcissism, or a defensive perspective—have the ability to work with others, they can collaborate to solve problems and innovate for success. This is why working on ourselves comes first and is an integral part of each stage of the development that follows.

A Commitment to Awaken

Since awakened individuals are aware of both their potential as a creative person and also of their shadow, they intentionally spend time developing their strengths and confronting their issues. Because they do this, they are able to align their actions with consciously chosen goals.

Awakened companies maintain the integrity of their own internal functioning and goals, while also intentionally participating in social, economic, and ecological environments that address needs beyond the basic function of the company.

An awakened executive is someone who is able to more deeply participate in the work of organizational support or leading, while remaining aware of his or her historic preferences and tendencies. This form of relationship work is all about working with ourselves so that we begin to recognize our pre-existing patterns. Such a leader is open to solutions or

modalities other than those they are used to and have traditionally relied upon. They can more easily call upon ways of
addressing challenges and issues with something other than
their tried and true default mechanisms.

It's a given that a self-aware leader encourages self-awareness in the entire team, which is why people report they prefer
to work with leaders who know the value of self-awareness.
An unawakened executive can really hold others back. As
one CEO realized, "The company was unable to grow until I
was able to evolve. In other words, I was the one holding the
company back. My personal growth is what finally enabled
the company to evolve."

It may be the case that a company doesn't have an awakened executive, but a few attributes are already in place or are
emerging in executives and the company as a whole. Perhaps
there are individuals who are already noticing their own patterns and unconscious habits. In this case, the formation of
a sub-group is recommended. You need a few people who
have awakened in themselves before you can create a team
of *awakeness*. And if you have people committed to a team
of awakeness, this helps the individuals to stay awake too—
rather like the way three or four logs in a fireplace support a
warming glow far more effectively than a single log.

This group of employees is committed to bringing greater
self-awareness and presence to their team, department, and
the entire company. They may all be working in the same
section or dispersed throughout the company. If the latter
is the case, informal get-togethers to gauge interest can be
helpful. Forming a meditation group or reading circle, with
being fully present and engaging in stress relief as the main
focus, would be a good starting point. The key is supporting

each other by coming together to cultivate awareness and talk about ways of increasing this among other employees, especially company executives.

An awakened community exudes respect and allowance for mystery within the self and the other. In such a relationship, we are quick to identify defenses that lead us away from authentic connection. While remaining aware of individual potential roadblocks to authentic engagement, an awakened community also provides ongoing opportunities for all parties to express their best qualities. In this process of growing self-awareness, we realize that it's through the magical alchemy of relationships that we learn and develop the most.

The quality of one's attentiveness to one's own process of self-discovery is also an important quality for companies. It's what enables a company to develop meaningful goals. When goals emerge from awareness, they don't have the effect of "hanging over us" in a burdensome manner that leads us to feel driven to accomplish them. The fact is, goals without awareness of a deeper purpose leave employees and management alike with a sense of meaninglessness. Such a feeling of meaninglessness is a malaise in many companies.

Although goals fulfill a helpful purpose in an awakened company, for awakened individuals they are tools, not the driving force behind the company. In an awakened company, goals are therefore likely to be more flexible. As our awareness increases, we may even abandon a goal, switching our purpose to something entirely different.

The goal-oriented voice in us may object, "What's the point if I can't achieve the goal I set?" But it's the actual experience of life's journey—the moments between our defined start and end points—that form our everyday lives, and therefore, matter most. Becoming truly present in each of the moments between these start and end points is the real goal.

To illustrate, someone born in 1965 who dies in 2023 has a start and end point. Between these two numbers on their tombstone is a dash. That small dash represents a lot of living, which is either significant or wasted. It isn't how we start out and finish that matters, but what we do in the in between—what we learn, accomplish, give, and share. Did we live our life with moral integrity during both the easy and challenging times, and did we learn important lessons?

An awakened company supports the cultivation and sustenance of the spacious functioning of its personnel. Consciously recognized and articulated goals are the aim. Instead of focusing on an end state, we recognize that all companies have the potential of becoming more intelligent, requiring an evolution of our goals. Since awakening to more refined states has no limits, this process is endless and thus provides endless opportunities.

7

PERSONAL DEVELOPMENT IS KEY

The principle barrier to establishing a healthy company culture is the attachment we each have to our particular self-image—"self-image" being the way we like to imagine ourselves, the picture of ourselves we carry around in our head.

When we are in high-stress, high-impact environments such as an office, factory, or governmental body, we often feel under pressure. In such a situation, we tend to maximally identify with our self-image, and hence, to promote it. This leads to a tunnel vision advancing of our own views at the expense of those of others. Simultaneously, we may be closed to options no one may yet have thought of, but that could potentially emerge from either truly open brainstorming, heart-storming, or further research.

Since, if we are deeply attached to our ego, it can be hard to let go of a concept we treasure, any real development requires us to challenge our concept of self, other, and the company as an entity. If we can let go of our attachment to seeing ourselves a certain way, this shift in how we perceive ourselves will in turn alter how we perceive and respond to our environment and the various challenging situations that arise in any line of work.

When we shelve our ego and consequently have no need to project our self-image into situations, we find ourselves no longer driven to effect a certain outcome. We have no ego investment in getting our way on a matter. By disengaging from our limited view, we become free to think, feel, and act in ways that break new ground. This allows for the emergence of a previously unimagined, and perhaps unimaginable, future for a company.

Since ego can be a stumbling block to growth of both the individual and the company, how are we to free ourselves from its clutches?

The Antidote to Ego

The antidote to ego is the practice highlighted in the previous chapter, involving a rigorous questioning of ourselves. Not the frenetic questioning in which the voices in our head are inclined to engage, but the kind of questioning that arises from a state of stillness. When we observe ourselves from a quiet questioning perspective, we begin to notice where we are holding ourselves back—and also undeveloped and perhaps hitherto undiscovered strengths, which show us where our growing edge is.

The kind of quiet self-observation and questioning I'm describing is poles apart from being critical of ourselves. All of us have an inner critic, and it can be vicious. Far from being an antidote to ego, the inner critic is one of the instruments of torture in the ego's dungeon. Its masochistic spirit is the *opposite* of what's required for constructive personal development. When the ego takes over an executive, a manager, a team leader, or a member of a team, it's entirely counterproductive, reducing people's effectiveness instead of enhancing it.

In contrast to an inner critic, there's nothing negative about self-questioning conducted in a spirit of self-observation. On the contrary, it's a pathway to making life fun, including our time at work. Investment banker, entrepreneur, philanthropist, and television personality W. Brett Wilson recognizes this and brings in personal coaches for himself and his team. They work together on understanding each other's personalities and ways of expressing themselves. As mentioned earlier, when we talked about Wilson's crew having the word "fun" in their titles, understanding each other's personalities helps foster a culture of love, respect, and *fun*.

Let's talk for a moment about what we mean by fun. "I think when there's respect, there's going to be an innate element of joy," Wilson says. Joy is bedrock in every human, if we only go deep enough to uncover it. It's an uncaused state that originates in our deepest being, and we tend to be particularly aware of it when our center is still.

While it's true that the bedrock of a serious but light work environment is joy, it needs to be pointed out that joy isn't the same as happiness and pleasure. Whereas happiness and pleasure arise in response to something that happens, joy is a more permanent state and can be experienced without any external stimulus. Given that some of the things we discover about ourselves when we self-observe aren't necessarily things that make us happy, it's extremely valuable to have tapped into our innate joy. When self-discovery takes place against a backdrop of inner joy, we can tolerate the discomfort of learning things about ourselves that need some work without such discoveries throwing us for a loop.

Joy is the fuel for our motivation to make real our ideas. It's because it's connected to the urge to create that it enables us to overcome pessimism, doubt, all manner of character flaws, and even failure. We feel a desire to celebrate the joy of being alive by making manifest what we have imagined: a better relationship, a better product or service, a better company, and even a better society.

In his book *The Science of Leadership*, Dr. Barling proposes that high quality leadership that's ethical, inspirational, developmental, and relational leads to followers who *question everything about themselves and yet are optimistic.*

Growing Together

As we touched on in the previous chapter, while each person is ultimately responsible for their own journey of self-discovery and self-development, paradoxically, this, in turn becomes one of the gifts we bring to our relationships within our working community.

As more of us come together with the intention of functioning consciously, it makes our individual development easier. In other words, the more we work on ourselves, the more we facilitate the group's ability to do this also. Consciousness is contagious.

To this end, a growing number of companies subscribe to the kind of philosophy espoused by Wilson of either enlisting professional help or encouraging practices that foster awareness in personnel. Such practices may range from keeping a journal to taking time to sit in stillness and simply breathe for several minutes each day.

To further illustrate the kinds of things that can be done, Joel Solomon of Renewal Funds says his lifelong journey to be more self-aware has included working with a variety of spiritual masters and teachers of awareness. "If I speak to business schools," he says, "a lot of times I get asked, 'What do you think is the single-most important thing for success in business?' And I say, 'Lifelong work on personal development and the inner skills.'" He urges everyone to find their own particular path to greater awareness.

Patagonia's Rose Marcario says meditation helps her bring focus to her business life, stating that she meditates every day and has for 20 plus years. "It's a big part of me," she says, "a way I get focused, gain perspective, calm my mind, and strengthen my heart."

Many of us have been brought up to think of focus as a kind of straining or "efforting" to pay attention. However, when I speak of "focus," I'm referring to a stabilization of our attention that arises as we become more grounded and, hence, calm. Sounds easy, but meditation practices have a way of revealing how difficult it is to sustain a focus for more than a short time. Consequently, to develop sustained focus requires a kind of mental calisthenics. In other words, training our attention requires the same kind of discipline and practice required to develop our physical body. The good news is that we can practice focusing our attention anywhere. While there are basic practices that take a few minutes a day, the ongoing work of noticing the quality of our attention can go on while we are engaged in our normal routine. People who train themselves to maintain their attention are generally more creative, more energized, and better both at listening and at communicating.

A study published in the *Journal of Corporate Citizenship* looked at managers at four European companies from the pharmaceutical industry, natural resources, and information technology. Researchers tested the effectiveness of various management education approaches designed to spur socially responsible behavior.

Traditional approaches to training in corporate social responsibility, based on explaining the importance of integrating more social and environmental concerns into their business, failed to change participants' decisions when they were faced with a dilemma involving corporate social responsibility. "On the other hand, approaches that involved mental silence, meditation, and relaxation techniques led to significant improvements in social consciousness and socially responsible behavior, even when CSR principles weren't actually mentioned. The meditating managers were more apt to prioritize social welfare over economic profit, and even more likely to prioritize protection of the natural environment over productivity. In addition, they had a greater overall sense of responsibility and inner harmony."[1]

This research invites us to consider completely redesigning leadership programs, along with many of our traditional executive development programs. If we are willing to reexamine what we have been taught and generally believe about how business best functions, we will discover that, while there are elements we wish to retain because they are proven to work, many of our practices are inefficient, outmoded, and were founded in times of war. These include rigid hierarchy and control, which are required in war, but which are largely inapplicable to life in normal times. During periods of conflict, we artificially boost an "us versus them" mentality, which fosters an unnecessarily combative spirit. The fact is, much of our leadership and business culture needs to be turned on its head.

Personally, I'm excited about additional studies on training methods that are currently underway in conjunction with Queen's University. These studies are breaking new ground, and this is just the beginning. As these studies proceed, it's already becoming clear that there are far more effective and simpler ways to train people for leadership in business than most of our companies are presently using.

In line with the aforementioned study in the *Journal of Corporate Citizenship,* Mac Van Wielingen of ARC Financial relates concerning his own experience, "I've had a meditation practice since I was probably 20 years of age. I practice meditation every morning. There have been periods when I didn't for a while, but I've been pretty disciplined about it and it's been very, very important to me. I would call it meditation-contemplation because often there are some readings involved. I might take from 20 minutes to an hour every morning. I get up early and always look forward to it. It's a critical practice."

In addition to bringing in professional help for his people, W. Brett Wilson also values meditation as a tool in the quest for wellbeing. He has developed a personal style of meditation. He explains, "I'd rather do four or five two-minute sessions of mindfulness in terms of bringing my mind back to center when it wanders. 'Oops! Squirrel. Bring it back.' There are many different forms of mindfulness. I just happen to like that concept of, 'Oops, bring it back.' And it does help you, in terms of clearing your head. You start out with a fresh slate. The dance floor is empty, whereas normally there's a football team out there, with a couple of lions, a tiger—all sorts of things running around on it."

Dave Logan,[2] author of the #1 bestseller *Tribal Leadership,* also appreciates the importance of meditation. "A lot comes down to personal development work," he says. "In my case, people sometimes comment that I seem very present. They want to know how I came to this. Well, it's been years of primarily meditation."

People who embody more of the qualities of awakened executives typically have some type of relaxation regimen like meditation or Tai Chi. They cultivate awareness by engaging in practices such as watching their dreams, participating in visualization, using guided imagery, reading poetry, or engaging in inspirational writing. As Wilson was saying, there are many different styles and methods that a person can employ. But like many things in life, the secret is to get started—to start experimenting with practices rather than just thinking about it.

The Value of Practicing Awareness Collectively

In addition to a personal investment in increasing awareness in companies, as already touched on, it can be helpful to take courses together involving inner development and psychological wholeness—courses like those offered by the Hoffman Institute or the Enneagram Institute, which encourage people to challenge their self-image and their habitual patterns to arrive at an expanded sense of themselves and their possibilities. Benefit can also be derived from conducting a 360-degree individual and cultural assessment that can be sent to a company's board of directors. More and more services specialize in supporting organizational development in these ways.

Joel Solomon says he's encouraged by the growth of yoga and meditation in the business world. Similarly, Mark Montemurro,[3] vice president at Baytex Energy, testifies, "I definitely know that yoga, the Enneagram, and coaching have all had an impact on the teams I have worked with. I know that because people will comment, in terms of the type of leadership style that I have. And if I were to characterize it, boil it down to two or three attributes, it would be transparency, trust, and open communication."

The Enneagram is an ancient system currently being used in leading professional services firms, Fortune 500 companies, and entrepreneurial organizations around the world. Based on an understanding of three fundamental types of intelligence—thinking, feeling, and instinct—its wisdom can be applied to relationships, teams, and organizations. The goal of the Enneagram is to free us from our habitual ways of acting, feeling, and thinking. One of my collaborators on this book has done much to further the use of the Enneagram in the world of business.

While many progressive companies send employees to courses, many also implement simple practices that help bring back focus and presence during the workday. A stillness break—taking a few moments to sit in silence before continuing to work—is a tool that helps employees make space by clearing their minds of previous conversations and activities in order to reset their focus on what's happening now. At BluEra, we gather in the boardroom in silence and reflect on our intentions for a short while. Sometimes we do this at the start of meetings, sometimes at the end, and at other times just to come together. Such breaks don't have to be long, but should be allowed to lengthen as the need arises and the organization matures.

Namaste Publishing's Constance Kellough believes that an editor's work is a reflection of their inner work. Her editors might be editing, but they are mindful, fully present in the task, instead of just doing a job. "In the end, you take who you *are* into what you *do*," she explains. "Everyone who works for Namaste Publishing is joined in oneness in our intent to bring the most highly conscious material to our readers. As such, we have attained and sustain a vital cohesiveness."

Otto Scharmer at MIT explains the importance of having a daily mindfulness practice: "Create a space for yourself, the space of stillness. And stillness means you basically let go of everything that isn't essential. You let go of all the noise, and you try to hone your attention to where your real intention is."

Scharmer goes on to reveal, "Mindfulness is close to reaching a tipping point. Only two years ago, mindfulness and mindful leadership were discussed at the WEF [World Economic Forum] for the first time. Since then, almost all of the mindfulness-related events there have been oversubscribed. Mindfulness practices like meditation are now used in technology companies such as Google and Twitter (among others), in traditional companies in the car and energy sectors, in state-owned enterprises in China, and in UN organizations, governments, and the World Bank." Other examples of companies using this approach are Aetna, General Mills, FaceBook, and eBay. These practices often have an impact on the bottom line, as seen with Aetna, which reduced its healthcare costs by 7%, attributed by the CEO, at least in part, to the introduction of meditation and yoga.[4] However, Bill Linton, CEO and founder of Promega, rejects the notion that adding yoga and meditation is all about making money, commenting that when everything is about the bottom line, it creates stress.[5]

As Loic Le Meur, a serial tech entrepreneur from Silicon Valley, puts it: "It's funny, everyone I know has started meditating."

8

HEALTHY COMPANIES FUNCTION FROM AWARENESS OF A HIGHER PURPOSE

Instead of "business is business," which implies that—as long as you make money—you can treat people any way you wish and get by with products of poor quality, more and more companies are discovering that a quite different slogan works for them.

That slogan is, "It pays to care." By this, I mean that it pays to provide real value to employees, clients, and all the stakeholders. Individuals who operate from this place know in a deep sense that their life has value. Ultimately, perhaps there's nothing more important than knowing our life has value, for this is what gives us meaning.

The recent financial meltdown was a huge cry for help from businesses using a model that's failing. Putting profit before people and the wider community that breathes life into a company may sometimes be expedient in some short term ways, but it has been clearly shown to be unsustainable. Of course, businesses do need to turn a profit; but when they value profit more than people, society, and the planet with its diverse life forms, the results can be disastrous. The thirst for "more" creates a special class of mercenary enterprise that all-too-often uses its power to defang regulations and aggressively engage in high-risk activity—to the detriment of society as a whole.

The nightly news details the surreal juxtaposition of a depressed economy, in which people are suffering, with the frantic accumulation of profits by a select few, revealing their lack of faith in an economy they helped to crash. Leading up to that crash, not all companies engaged in the worst behaviors, but many were on their way to losing their corporate soul.

In contrast to this mentality of greed, awakened executives are often willing to sacrifice personal gain for the sake of others. They put the company vision and sense of the larger mission they are supporting ahead of their own interests. Instead of using their power for personal advantage, they use it to move the team toward accomplishing a vision that benefits not only the company, but also the wider world.

It needs to be said that the awakened executive knows *when* to sacrifice themselves for others and their cause, *as well as when not to*. They sense when sacrifice is mostly for public consumption, as opposed to when it can make a real difference in the lives of others. They also know *what* to sacrifice. There's no sacrificing of health, integrity, or wellbeing, each of which are true needs. Instead, awakened executives are able to forgo wants that aren't essential to fulfillment but have more to do with show. To illustrate, my business partner and I didn't take a salary for two years when we founded BluEra. What made this worthwhile was the knowledge we were creating something so different, so meaningful to us, that it would eventually have a very positive impact. Our souls weren't going hungry during this period.

It's for this reason that developing our self-awareness

needs to include awareness of our motives. As well as inquiring about our true needs, we also inquire about our true aims. Our purpose isn't to reject any egoic or materialist motives outright, but rather to be unabashedly honest with ourselves so we can tune into our truest and most fulfilling aims. When we do so, we are also less quick to judge others' motives or to make unsupported assumptions about their needs.

The Prevalence and Persistence of the Profit Mantra

Despite the nightmare that resulted from the unscrupulous business practices that led to the crash of 2008, the "profit above all" mantra that threatens employee security, the economy, and the environment is still prevalent. Far too many businesses frequently lay off employees, then outsource work to countries with cheap labor and lax regulations in terms of product quality, protecting the environment, and caring for their laborers.

This "profit above all" mentality is why many turned a blind eye to the conditions of near slavery at Foxconn, the world's largest electronics contractor manufacturer, which had suicide nets around the factory to prevent workers from jumping to their death. This was a company assembling products for major American, European, and Japanese electronics firms, including the Kindle, BlackBerry, iPad, iPhone, Playstation 4, Xbox One, and Wii U.

It should also be pointed out that neither did anyone in the business community stand up before more than a thousand Bangladeshis, mostly women, were killed in a garment factory fire that manufactured cheap clothing for the North American market.

Most overlooked is how widespread and accepted these horrific conditions have become. Somehow we have normalized these types of practices as acceptable business behavior, even when we know it creates destructive situations, not just for the workers themselves, but for humanity as a whole. Yes, it's better for eight workers to sleep in a dormitory than a dozen, but is such a dormitory existence really acceptable in this day and age? Can a company, in any sense, claim to be "awake" and expect workers to live this way day in and day out?

What an opportunity this is for the world's most successful companies to set a precedent by taking their vast profits and, instead of luxuriating them on shareholders, transforming the workplaces in which products are manufactured into venues we can all be proud of and that those who make these wonderful products can enjoy. If you are a corporation, are you ready to lead the way in bringing joy to the workers who, in countries such as China, assemble the stellar products brought to the service of humanity? At this juncture, no one else could pull off the kind of world-shaking paradigm shift that major incorporations are in a position to trigger.

The excessive profit mantra deadens the heart, rendering it challenging for the participants to awaken to a kinder way of doing business. When we close off our heart, we disable our higher intelligence, which includes wisdom, empathy, and compassion. We are unable to sense our natural interconnection with and dependence upon the people, creatures, and ecosphere around us. It isn't that we would choose to create harm for others; we just don't want to know. But such willed ignorance can only have a devastating effect on our awareness across the board, with subsequent shutting down of our optimal creativity and intelligence.

Comments Renewal Funds' Joel Solomon, "We have built a lot of modern wonders for humanity and civilization, using human ingenuity and cleverness to find ways to make a washing machine so we don't have to hand-wash our clothes in the river, automobiles and airplanes to transport us, and computers and telephones to enable us to communicate. But in the process of going from living tribal, living on the land as hunter-gatherers, to agriculture and now to the modern economy, we've left behind the spiritual understanding of where this all comes from. The moral and ethical aspects have been neutralized, so that hardly anyone is asking when enough is enough. The one thing you can pretty much guarantee, is that if you ask people what they want in terms of money, it's the four-letter word 'more.'"

Bringing this back to the workplace, Solomon says, "The workplace is the day-to-day acting out of these grand energies and societal truths—the agreed-upon understandings we've even forgotten we agreed on, which are that we'll behave in a certain way. Depending on where we are in the pecking order of the power structure of a workplace, we may see injustice, inconsistency, and a gross lack of awareness. But then we are given more responsibility. Suddenly we find ourselves in a system that answers to quarterly bottom lines and shareholders, and we gradually buy into this way of thinking. We are the stewards of these workplaces, making decisions about people's lives—about what the workplace looks like, what you can talk about, and what the culture is."

Interconnected and Interdependent

In an awakened company, everyone in the company understands that they are simultaneously interconnected and interdependent. All of the individuals that constitute the company are aware that each member—as stated earlier, from the CEO to the financial and operations crew, as well as the maintenance crew—plays a vital role in sustaining the organization. There's an awareness that reciprocity is a fundamental feature of healthy systems. For the most part, every employee knows they are responsible to each other, the community, and the ecosphere, with each part relying on the other for a balanced and prosperous life. This harmonious way of being in the world tends to buoy each employee's heart.

When these values are in place in a company, there arises a sense of having a higher purpose—of being part of something greater than a machine that generates profit, as well as greater than the individual tasks and components employees normally focus on.

When an organization has this sense of a greater purpose, it naturally fosters in the people in it a readiness to shoulder the responsibility it implies. When people create organizations more consciously—aware of the greater context, their purpose, and mutual support—they begin to function more like intelligent organisms in which the total system is "smarter" than the sum of its individual parts. This phenomenon is popularly called "synergy." Awakened companies develop and cultivate such synergy, with the diverse components or systems in the company each influencing and improving the other. This synergy isn't an artificial construct, but reflects something of how natural systems work, and is only possible because we are already all interconnected at some deeper level.

On the way to this synergy, individuals who interact reciprocally become aware of being part of larger systems, and each of these systems has, if you will, its own ecology—the elements that support its existence and wellbeing. We come to see that systems affect larger systems of which they are a part, with a two-way flow from larger to smaller and smaller to larger. Thus the individual's personal ecology affects the team and corporate ecology, and the corporate ecology affects the larger ecology of the society and its wellbeing—and even the literal ecology of nature.

The awakened company is led by executives who realize that employees' wellbeing and society's wellbeing are inextricably linked to the company's long-term wellbeing. The understanding and nurturing of this interrelationship becomes part of the company's bottom line, so that such responsibilities as maintaining a healthy ecosystem become factors in our corporate wealth equation—since if the ecosystem fails, the human economy fails.

Once we discover that compassion breeds success, we are eager to adopt an expanded definition of success that includes more than the bottom line. Executives who cultivate compassion and encourage this in their employees are making one of the most sound investments a business can make. What may be surprising to many is that corporate financial health and wealth are not sacrificed in this way of doing business. On the contrary, corporate profitability becomes both more likely and more enduring. Indeed, companies that engage in "conscious capitalism" perform ten times better than traditional companies.[1]

Clearly, it pays to care and become self-aware.

A Sacred Business

When we awaken, we realize we are more than our thoughts, emotions, and behavior. We sense a dignity and beauty within ourselves, a valuing of ourselves that extends to the whole of humanity and, indeed, the entire planet. We feel a connection with everyone and everything. This feeling of connection spawns a sense of our inherent sacredness and the sacredness of life as a whole—the kind of sacredness that touches our hearts when we look at the night sky or at our children at play. It's a direct sense that there is something good about this world and about this life. As this feeling of sacredness flows into our work, we act from a deeper place within us. Our awareness of our sacredness promotes empathy and compassion for a wider and wider circle.

As this awareness of our deep connection increases, it expresses itself as a greater desire to help and support others. This comes quite naturally because, now when we help another, it feels like we are helping ourselves. When we share with another, we feel we are sharing with a greater part of ourselves. A natural reciprocity arises, reflecting an awareness that our own wellbeing and success depend on the wellbeing and success of the other. It's this heartfelt connection that imbues each person and moment with a sense of sacredness, so that each perceives the relationship as precious and not to be dishonored.

From this more holistic perspective that's arising in those companies that have caught onto this, we develop a higher sense of purpose for ourselves with respect to our fellow humans. We feel part of a bigger picture, and we want to contribute to it. This becomes something more than a sense of duty; indeed, we recognize that much of the feeling of meaning in our lives comes this way. Because we are involved with helping others not only to end their struggle simply to survive, but also to maximize their enjoyment of life, we do everything in our power to assist them to grow and thrive along with us. Deep fulfillment not only for ourselves, but also for those around us becomes a priority.

As Tony Robbins comments, "We all know there are many kinds of wealth: emotional wealth; relationship wealth; intellectual wealth; physical wealth, in the form of energy, strength, and vitality; and, of course, spiritual wealth: the sense that our life has a deeper meaning, a higher calling beyond ourselves. One of the biggest mistakes we human beings make is when we focus on mastering one form of wealth at the expense of all the rest."[2]

Align Yourself with Your Purpose

As a higher purpose than merely working for our own benefit takes hold of us, we feel a need to align our new personal values with the work we do. Our highest potential will be achieved through the values that remain when the mask of our ego falls away. Most of us are amazed at how our deepening awareness actually brings the fulfillment we have been looking for in other ways.

For Patagonia's Rose Marcario, aligning personal and business values became essential. She recalls that she "was working for an investment bank doing mergers and acquisitions and doing big transactions, so I was making a lot of money, but I wasn't really fulfilled."

What changed things? "I ended up studying Buddhism when I was in Silicon Valley and became very involved in that practice. It started to become clear to me that I wanted to work in a way that was aligned with my values. So it was a sort of early mid-life crisis, and it caused me to really reflect."

Today, Marcario says, "I work with just an amazing team of people and we really share the values. I think that's what makes the company great, the people, and the values."

Our friend Robert Holden, a British motivational writer, psychologist, and broadcaster, has made his life's work having people ask and answer the kind of questions Marcario found herself asking—questions such as, "Is this really what will make me happy? Is it truly what success is for me? Is it what success is for this company? Does it reflect my heart and the hearts in the company?"

When our personal values are aligned with our work, we create a working life for ourselves that's about more than making money. It's about the experience itself. Constance Kellough of Namaste Publishing exemplifies this. "Each step of the way, it has been important not to allow ego to affect our business decisions," she says. "Our purpose has never been to become a large publishing concern, but simply to provide an avenue for Presence to raise the consciousness of our fellow humans."

Once we recognize we have a purpose that extends to our company, and through our company to the wider world, success as a company means making life better for our employees, their families, and our clientele. This in turn creates a better world for everyone.

Craig Kielburger, cofounder of Me To We, a social enterprise whose work projects around the world empower people, feels that involving his employees directly in the higher purpose of the organization helps create a humane company culture. He speaks of "ensuring that we connect the mission and role as clearly as possible to people."

One way in which Me To We achieves this is to do a staff

trip every two years. Kielburger explains, "It doesn't matter whether you are a receptionist or janitorial staff. Everyone has the opportunity to go on a volunteer trip to see the projects and understand how their work connects to these projects."

At Matrix, to nourish and evolve the company, Rob Pockar realized they had to first define their purpose, which involved a branding exercise and identifying their place in the market. "We decided that our purpose was to have our people, our communities, our clients, and the environment thrive— and we think about all four of those as communities, really," Pockar explains.

Beyond the intrinsic rewards, extensive research shows that companies with a higher purpose are also highly profitable.[3] Pockar attests to this, stating, "I attended a conference where we compiled data from about 250 different environmental and engineering consulting firms, and our company is top quartile, both in respect of profitability and internal growth. So we are a high-performing company." Pockar concludes that what's driven this high performance has been the company's "culture" along with "that work on purpose and that work on alignment."

Even with regard to the day-to-day functioning of our work world, work need not be about simply checking off the tasks, but rather about getting things done in a heartfelt way, since being driven to check off tasks can lead to a sense of detachment from one's true self and higher purpose. It's a matter of realizing, as stated earlier, that goals aren't the only reason for working. In fact, movement toward a goal can become a kind of mechanized, unconscious, non-stop activity in which larger visions and deeper purposes are ignored. When goal attainment dominates, there's a loss of awareness of a greater context and moral responsibility. The adrenalized tunnel vision that takes over in order to hit certain targets comes at the expense of individual, company, and community wellbeing. We lose our own personal sense of fulfillment, and company morale declines along with the loss of purpose and direction. This kind of behavior has driven companies and entire economies over the cliff.

For this reason, it's essential companies ask themselves *why* they have a particular goal, and whether it aligns with their greater purpose in life. We are here to understand who we really are and what the work of our life is, so that we live with purpose, value, and meaning. Without this deeper perspective, the experience of satisfaction we all desire becomes elusive.

Meaning Is a Matter of an Engaged Heart

When our work isn't fulfilling, we inevitably suffer. The pandemic of unsatisfying labor is one of the principle reasons so many on our planet are suffering.

ARC Financial's Mac Van Wielingen explains, "Suffering doesn't necessarily mean you're down and out, or you're on the street. Suffering shows itself as meaninglessness. It will show itself as having a sense of worthlessness—the feeling you don't have value. It will also show up as a feeling of powerlessness, whereby you feel insignificant."

Meaning is a function of the heart. We might work competently and accomplish many things; but if our heart isn't really in what we are doing, the work will feel hollow and meaningless. Even when we are doing interesting and potentially fulfilling work, if we aren't truly engaged in what we are doing, with our heart deeply involved, we will feel deprived of meaning in our life. You can see this from the number of highly "successful" people who become depressed or even suicidal, despite the acclaim they experience in their career. Without heart involvement, what we do can't nourish our spirit, despite the fact that what we are doing is beneficial to others.

Even the seemingly insignificant moments have significance when our heart is involved. Minor events are seen as precious when we are engaged with the experience. To foster such engagement, see if you can find the joy in the simple accomplishment of any task you are performing. For instance, when you perform a normally routine physical task such as cleaning, washing the dishes, vacuuming, or mowing the lawn, engage it a little more slowly than you usually would, tuning into your heart as you give focused attention to the physical actions involved in the task. What do you notice that's different from how you usually engage tasks? Let yourself experience the raw amazingness of the moment.

We tend to notice when people are checked-out, distracted, bored. Neither does it take great insight to see that much of the modern propensity for distraction is a desperate effort to avoid feelings of meaninglessness. However, what may not be so obvious is that people can be energetic and active, yet not really engaged.

Genuine engagement has its foundations in groundedness, which is a relaxed state. This is fundamentally different from the driven state from which many of us operate. Were we to take a snapshot of our inner self while we are working, many of us would see how our stressful trains of thought actually disconnect us from our environment.

In our work life, where we are most in need of being grounded, we are often least likely to take the opportunity to reconnect with ourselves. We become accustomed to operating in a highly stressful, frenetic, ungrounded mode—which may produce results, but at a cost that's high and not sustainable over the long haul.

As individuals, it helps to take moments throughout our workday to breathe, feel our feet on the ground, and catch up with ourselves. This brings a crispness to our attention, which in turn fosters confidence. Groups and teams can build in moments to pause, so that instead of charging right back into hyperactivity, they re-engage tasks from greater groundedness. Such groundedness is a precursor to feeling connected.

When we feel connected, we feel supported, which is why meaning is closely related to feelings of appreciation and gratitude. The result is engagement, which is energizing. We feel like we are more deeply inhabiting the process, which makes the work so much more satisfying.

9

TRUST

Traditionally, we've been taught to put our trust in contracts for our business dealings. However, awakened executives inspire us to trust something deeper.

Matrix's Robert Pockar sees *trusting one's colleagues* as essential in the creation of a "really humane workplace." This trust involves empowering them by providing freedom and flexibility. As Pockar asserts, "If you give people the opportunity to make a wise decision that's fair to them, their clients, and the company, they will make it. They will make wise decisions."

Zappos shares this same philosophy. "Trust is a key ingredient for success at Zappos," says Jamie Naughton.

Expounding on the theme of trust, Pockar adds that to trust one's colleagues is to hold an "underlying belief people can accept that with the flexibility comes great responsibility. We believe people can manage that responsibility."

Spelling out what his company's belief in people means in practice, Pockar explains, "The way we create our compensation program, the way we create our benefits program, the way we run our training, and the way we delegate work is based on the notion that our people can be given choices and options. They can be given the authority to accept assignments or walk away from assignments, set their hours, and set their reimbursability."

In contrast to this, there are instances of companies pulling back from trust in their employees, reining in employees who have been used to working at home, believing many to be abusing the privilege.

The leadership lesson is that among the extremes in business, a middle harmonious way exists. There's a delicate balance between being naïve and being trusting. Trust requires an act of faith that inspires all of us to live in truth. This means a culture of openness, involving being able to talk about bad news and stepping into dialogue to hold each other accountable.

If personnel who are supposed to be working as telecommuters aren't investing sufficient time, it may be that a shift away from trusting employees reflects the company's failure to nurture a culture in which individuals are aware of and invested in the organization's higher purpose. Even if they come into the office, they may show up at the job, but they don't bring their whole self to work.

In other words, the problem is a lack of buy-in—either because the wrong people are in the wrong jobs, or because the company has failed to excite them and engage them in its mission. To reiterate Pockar's insight, it's about purpose, and alignment with this purpose. When purpose is clearly understood, it becomes a simple matter of placing people where they can serve effectively.

When an executive feels under the gun, overwhelmed, stressed, or in need of demonstrating his or her leadership ability, they may claim that what's being accomplished by an organization is adequate. Consequently, they resist different modes of working, new projects, and innovation.

This kind of resistance generates office politics and disharmony, with the result that the team loses its sense of proactive optimism. The leader's fear that others aren't shouldering their share of the work then becomes a self-fulfilling prophecy.

The preferable way is for executives to be open about their feelings. If colleagues really aren't carrying their weight, this should be discussed and not used as an excuse by the executive to overextend themselves or to say "no" to new projects or work practices.

Mac Van Wielingen believes that whereas there's so much disgruntlement and discord in companies, we should actually be able to find peace in our places of business. Spelling out what he means by this, he states, "If we can in a sense hold each other in our relationships with sensitivity, gentleness, tenderness, affection, in a way that's affirming, we create a sense of safety for people on a personal level. With that sense of safety comes a letting go of guardedness and defensiveness, so that there's more ease. People are more relaxed, more themselves. There's a sense of equanimity in that, a feeling of peace."

A Healthy Company Culture Is Grounded in Trust

Trust, openness, honesty, mutual respect, and flexibility are the recurring themes within the company cultures we have explored.

Kent Brown,[1] President, CEO, and Director of BluEarth Renewables, comments, "The ability for employees to come and go as they please creates a sense of peace."

At BluEra, we instituted unlimited vacation time because we trust the people we work with. This allows them the space to do what needs to be done in their own time. IBM, Netflix, and many other companies have gotten rid of traditional vacation policies.

Michael Mahoney adds, "By tossing the two-week standard in favor of an honor system with unlimited time off, some companies are seeing an exponential rise in productivity. Now, they just have to be mindful of staff burnout."

Constance Kellough at Namaste Publishing also adheres to these principles, working with her colleagues with a trust and respect that allows for great autonomy. "They are all independent," she says. "They're self-monitoring and they're responsible. They are the managers of their area of responsibility. It's empowering for them. They can be very creative within that area—and all of them are. They're growing their areas in enlightened and progressive ways. I have faith in them, and this allows Namaste Publishing that kind of flexibility."

Kellough says of her team, all of whom telecommute, with only herself in the central office, "They can take vacations whenever they want. The irony is they take very few. And when they do take them, they often work regardless, so that I have to tell them not to. I have said, 'You're working too hard. I'm not adding another project at this time, so that you go easy on yourself.'"

Says Lydia Dishman, "Worker bees may be buzzing happily, but eventually everyone needs a real break. That's why the 17-year-old Motley Fool, a multimedia financial-services company, established 'The Fool's Errand' five years ago. Spokesperson Alison Southwick says it's a monthly ritual where, at a meeting of all 250 employees, one name is drawn from a hat. That person must take off two consecutive weeks sometime in the ensuing month. Southwick says its purpose is twofold. 'First, it helps make sure that people are taking time off, clearing their heads, and recharging their batteries. Second, it helps us fight against single points of failure within the company. When you suddenly take two weeks off, you need to make sure that other people around you understand what you do so that the company doesn't come to a screeching halt if you're gone,' she explains."[2]

Michael Mahoney agrees that unlimited vacation fosters productivity and loyalty because it favors results over input, says Dishman. In the final analysis, it isn't time spent on the job that counts, but what's actually achieved.

Interviewing Sir John Templeton, one of the true geniuses of investing as well as one of the great philanthropists of the 20th century, Tony Robbins asked, "Sir John, most people seem to be either money oriented or spiritually oriented— they have to be one or the other—but you seem to have found a way to integrate these two in a truly natural and real way in your life. Can people integrate both in their lives?"

Here, quoted by Tony Robbins, is Sir John Templeton's insightful response:

> Definitely! There is no disparity. Would you want to deal with a businessman you could not trust? No! If a man has a reputation for not being trustworthy, people will run away from him. His business will fail. But if another man has high ethical principles, he will try to give to his customers and his employees more than they expect. If so, he

will be popular. He will have more customers. He will make more profit. He will do more good in the world, and thereby he will prosper himself and have more friends and be more respected.

So always start out to give more than is expected from you, to treat the other person more fairly, and that is the secret of success. Never try to take advantage of anyone or hold anyone back in their own progress. The more you help others, the more prosperous you will be personally.[3]

GIVING BACK IS THE FUTURE

The desire to create a more humane business often coincides with the desire to be a force for good in the world. This reflects the higher purpose we feel emerging inside us as a result of greater self-awareness. Such increased self-awareness eventually expands to include the surrounding community and the world as a whole—and this has a positive influence on the company culture.

Says world-renowned speaker and teacher, business coach, and philanthropist Tony Robbins in his book *Money— Master the Game,* "The ultimate message of this book is very simple....The final secret of wealth is: the secret to living is giving."[1]

It's for this reason that awakening leaders and their businesses—including many giants in the business world—are increasingly finding ways to express gratitude for and show compassion toward both the communities and ecology that support their company's existence. For instance, many businesses that were built on accumulating wealth are now discovering how fulfilling it is to contribute in tangible ways to the wellbeing of others.

Caring for the Environment

Rose Marcario at Patagonia is on board with this. "One of the things we do is give one percent every year of our sales to grassroots environmental organizations. Although these are usually smaller grants in the $10,000 to $20,000 range, a lot of them go to the causes we care about, which revolve around energy, water conservation, and wildlife preservation. We want to protect both the land and the diversity of species, so we support folk who are dealing with toxins in their water and issues of waste. As Yvon Chouinard, founder of Patagonia, would say, 'We pay our earth tax every year through this program.' We also fund a program that enables our employees to work with any environmental organization for a few weeks a year. All they need to do is come back and report on their trip for the rest of the group. We let people go work on issues that are important to them. For example, when the oil spill in the Gulf of Mexico occurred, we had employees teamed with an NGO. We paid their salaries while they performed the work. We also match our employees' contributions to environmental organizations 100%, as well as hosting events in our stores to support local environmental organizations."

China's Alibaba.com recently passed both eBay and Amazon as the world's largest e-commerce company. It's heartening to discover that major Chinese companies are changing the way they do business. For instance, concern for the earth has prompted Alibaba to earmark 0.3% of their annual revenue for environmental "awareness, conservation, and remedial actions."[2]

Jack Ma, founder and chairman of Alibaba Group, strongly encourages employees "to develop and be active in environment-friendly programs." In an effort to foster a more democratic working environment, Ma has employees elect representatives "who determine how the company spends its annual philanthropy budget."[3] Measures such as these have a major impact on motivation and commitment.

Although Ma remains chairman of Alibaba Group, he recently stepped down as Chief Executive to focus on making the world a better place, especially when it comes to the environment. In a written piece, he explains, "Our water has become undrinkable, our food inedible, our milk poisonous, and worst of all the air in our cities is so polluted that we often cannot see the sun. Twenty years ago, people in China were focusing on economic survival. Now, people have better living conditions and big dreams for the future. But these dreams will be hollow if we cannot see the sun."

In his book *Money*, Tony Robbins draws our attention to Paul Tudor Jones. Not only is he the founder of Tudor Investment Corporation, but he founded the Robin Hood Foundation, which has become an inspiration to many. Says Jones concerning the environment, "Financial stress right now for me is that there are so many causes that I believe in. My financial stress relates to being able to give to the things that make me happy, that create passion in my life, and that are really exciting. There's a huge conservation project that I've just discovered about a month ago that I probably can't afford. The time frame on this is 100 years, at least. And I'm thinking, 'Oh my God! If I went and bought this timber operation, and let that land heal, and restored it. One hundred years from that day—it's going to be one of the most breathtakingly beautiful places! This is where God would have spoken to Adam; it has to be the Garden of Eden.' And

I'm thinking, 'Okay, I can't afford it, but I really want to do it. I better go out and work my ass off, because it will be the best contribution I can make to someone one hundred years from now.' They won't know who did it, but they'll love that spot and they'll be so happy."[4]

Caring for Humanity at Large

PMC's W. Brett Wilson is a believer in community service. "We take our entire office to Mexico every two years to build homes," he says. "Every year we volunteer at one of the churches to feed the hungry."

Community service is also a core value at Zappos, where employees are encouraged to volunteer their time for a variety of causes and are paid for the hours they volunteer.[5]

Microsoft, Timberland, and Eli Lilly & Company are other examples of the growing business trend of providing paid time off to employees who volunteer locally and abroad.[6]

Google's emphasis on employee self-awareness includes their connection to the world around them. For instance, "The company's Donations for Doers program encourages volunteerism by donating $50 for every five hours a Googler volunteers with an approved nonprofit."[7] They also have an annual global event, GoogleServe. Since 2008, this employee-driven initiative has seen Google employees around the world take a week in June to give back to communities everywhere. In 2013, more than 8,500 Googlers from 75+ offices participated in 500 projects. The projects Google employees participated in that year include leading a workshop on media literacy in Bhutan, spearheading a bone marrow drive in California, helping children with cognitive disabilities in

India, cooking meals for families with children undergoing cancer treatment in London, England, and walking the streets of New York City gathering information to improve the AXS Map platform that maps wheelchair accessibility.[8]

More and more companies don't need to be convinced of the benefits of helping their community and the planet. Zappos CEO Tony Hsieh now consults with other businesses on the effects of charity work on employee satisfaction and engagement. Not only does volunteer work aid in learning new skills and personal growth, but his consultancy website asserts that "paying employees to do charity work in the local community can increase their job satisfaction." An additional benefit is that it's "an effective way of increasing employee engagement in the workplace," which is "a very important factor in an organization's success."[9]

Craig and Marc Kielburger created social enterprise Me to We as a funding vehicle for their charity Free the Children. The latter's educational and development programs have impacted millions of children in over 45 countries. Not only are the Kielburgers committed to freeing children from poverty and exploitation, but they also seek to rid children of the notion that young people have no power to make a difference in the world.[10] Me to We gives half its profits to Free The Children, while using the other half to expand its own social mission, which includes making people more socially and environmentally conscious as consumers, developing community leaders, and creating exploitation-free jobs for the creators of the books and artisanal products they sell.

When it comes to Paul Tudor Jones' concern for poverty, he has been called a modern-day Robin Hood. Especially inspiring is the investors Jones has been able to involve in his

Robin Hood Foundation, along with the board's participation. Tony Robbins comments, "As the founder of the iconic Robin Hood Foundation, Jones has inspired and enrolled some of the smartest and wealthiest investors in the world to attack poverty in New York City. Paul and the Robin Hood team do this work with the same analytical rigor that hedge fund billionaires typically reserve for financial investments. Since 1988, Robin Hood has invested over $1.45 billion in city programs. And just like Jones's relentless pursuit of asymmetric return in his financial life...his foundation work is not different. Robin Hood's operating and administrative costs are covered 100% by board participation, so donors earn 15-1 return on their investment in their community! As Eric Schmidt, executive chairman of Google, says, 'There is literally no foundation, no activity, that is more effective.'"[11]

Measuring the Real Bottom Line

Social enterprises like Me to We emphasize people and planet over profit.

As cofounder Craig Kielburger told us, "We measure the bottom line, not by dollars earned, but by the number of lives we change and the positive social and environmental impacts we make."[12]

Me to We walk their talk when helping humans and the environment by keeping in mind that their efforts must empower people without overburdening the environment. "We realized that the very act of running the social enterprise could be socially conscious," Kielburger explains. "In other words, it's not just about the profits generated, but how we went about generating those profits." He adds that from carbon offsetting all of their international volunteer trips, shipping, and domestic travel, to printing on recycled paper and avoiding all pesticides in the production of their products, Me to We is committed to leaving "a light footprint on the earth."[13]

To date, Me to We has helped plant more than 667,000 trees to offset their international travels and to reforest places like Kenya, where they build schools and rebuild communities.[14] As part of this community building, Me to We provides full-time employment to 800 African artisans affectionately known as the "Masai Mamas." Their crafts, and many other Me to We products, are all ethically manufactured.

Dr. Hande's SELCO Solar also focuses on lowering environmental impact, while simultaneously helping to empower the poor. SELCO's goal isn't to maximize profit above all else, but to be a financially and socially sustainable company that cares for the long-term wellbeing of its employees and clients. SELCO was born of a desire to help the poorest in society achieve self-sufficiency in an environmentally conscious manner.

From the outset, the company was confident a business model that empowered customers could be viable. In fact, SELCO was conceived to dispel three myths associated with sustainable technology and the rural sector as a target customer base: the belief that poor people can't afford sustainable technologies, that poor people can't maintain sustainable technologies, and that social ventures can't be run as commercial entities. SELCO employs nearly 300 people across five Indian states and has "sold, serviced, and financed over 150,000 solar systems."[15]

Toward an Awakened Economy

Many of the business experts and leaders we interviewed are fully aware that our current economic model is unsustainable. Suggesting we need to change the underlying financial structure of society, Rose Marcario put her finger on the core issue: "This really comes from my experience of working in it and doing it myself for many years, but the idea that you're going to invest money and get a twenty-fold return in five years isn't a healthy model. It doesn't create jobs, and neither does it build lasting companies that make good products and stand behind them. Instead, it feeds greed." She adds that "if you look at what happened in 2006 to 2008, with the financial crisis and the total destruction of the markets, it was all based on just plain greed."

W. Brett Wilson of PMC agrees. "Go back to 2007, 2008. People said there was a credit crisis. I saw it as a crisis of morality. It was a morality based on greed." Why did the crisis occur? "It wasn't because people were paying too much for their homes. It was because the infrastructure was set up to allow that. When people believe they are above accountability, above reporting, that's a crisis of morality."

The resulting poverty and social instability from this crisis is eating away at the foundations of society and the environment that sustain us. Thus companies engaging in the kind of behavior that led to this crisis are placing their own financial sustainability at risk.

It's in everyone's interest to end the kind of corporate greed that does nothing to rid our species of poverty. As Dr. Hande explains, "Repeated studies around the world show that maps of conflict zones and those of energy and economic poverty overlap." He adds, "The social sustainability that we speak of—the basic ecosystem fabric required for all businesses to flourish—is threatened by the very existence of poverty."[16]

If any part of us still wants to believe that "business is business," we might want to think long and hard about what our company is currently contributing to—and what it potentially could be as a powerful and much-needed force for change.

11

CORPORATE SOCIAL RESPONSIBILITY

"The biggest challenge that business and organizations face today has many names but one common denominator," declares MIT's Otto Scharmer. "The names I use are the ecological divide, the social divide, the cultural divide, and the spiritual divide."

All of these forces—ecological, social, cultural, and spiritual—are merely people emphasizing different roles and needs. However, as we become more self-aware, our habitual roles start to loosen their grip on our identity, which leads to rediscovery of our common humanity.

As Scharmer goes on to explain, "The common denominator is what matters, which is that no single organization or sector alone can ever solve these issues. It's impossible. We need to reach out and to develop collaborative relationships, co-creating realities across institutional boundaries and across sector boundaries."

From the collective disgust at some recent business behavior, to the calls for changing the way our youth are educated about business and the trend toward personal growth and humane company cultures, there are indications we are in the throes of a movement toward a new kind of economy based on this rediscovery of our common humanity.

A Changing World

To illustrate the kind of change that's underway, witness the fact that in the United States alone there are hundreds of social enterprises, with more than 11,000 companies owned either entirely or to a significant degree by some 13.6 million employees. More than one in three Americans have an affiliation with a co-operative, while 1.6 million non-profit corporations often cross over into economic activity. Additionally, tens of thousands of businesses and professionals are members of councils and alliances that promote sustainable economic practices.[1]

There also appears to be a growing trend among for-profits to behave more like non-profits, whereas non-profits are increasingly behaving like for-profits. The rise of social enterprises indicates that some non-profits have seen the limits of their model and are trying to be more efficient by adding a measure of for-profit behavior.

For example, as successful as Free The Children has been, it wasn't long before Craig and Marc Kielburger realized the limits of the charity model. Craig recounts one of the defining moments in moving from a purely charitable model to one that included a social enterprise. "Marc and I were in Sierra Leone, where we'd been doing Free The Children projects for a decade at the time. Now it's well over a decade. We were waiting for a medical supply shipment at the docks and talking to a fellow relief worker we respected, asking what he was willing to ship in. He explained that he was shipping out. The dollars had dried up. No one was focused on Sierra Leone, since it wasn't on the front pages of the newspaper anymore. So they decided to leave and go to the next crisis that was on the front page. A lot of the non-profit world lurches from crisis to crisis. Whatever is on the front page of newspapers is where donors give, and therefore where non-profits tend to follow. We were fearful of the idea that we would run out of funding for our projects in Sierra Leone, and frankly also angered at the idea that so often the non-profit world was forced to leave half-finished projects and not to invest where there's the greatest need." It was as a result of this experience that Marc and Craig created social enterprise Me to We as a funding mechanism that could sustain Free The Children's charity work. This is a beautiful example of business savvy applied to larger issues through an awakened leader.

Similarly, Patagonia's Rose Marcario was quick to recognize that a drive toward a new economy must include more than for-profits and non-profits. It must include all stakeholders in society. For this reason, when the Benefit Corporation legislation was introduced, requiring companies to identify things that are equally important to them as financial returns for their shareholders, Patagonia was the first to register. Explaining her reasoning, Marcario comments, "I don't think we're going to change the world with NGOs and not-for-profits. I believe that they're really important and that they have a place, but the biggest force for change, I think, is really business."

The reality is that current trends are taking all organizations—for-profit and non-profit—in the same direction, which is toward more socially and environmentally responsible behavior. We have seen abundant proof that the unawakened individual and company, based in ego, is fearful, greedy, and negativity-prone, and that in this state we are incapable of running even our personal lives for our ultimate wellbeing, let alone running the planet—as can be seen in the individual suffering we all face and the collective suffering that could be heading us toward planetary disaster.

Can Business Save the World?

In our interviews with Hande, Mintzberg, and Wilson, they helped us reflect on the idea of corporate social responsibility. These visionary leaders have also helped us see that such responsibility isn't an "extra," either for individuals or for companies.

"I'm really tired of this term 'corporate social responsibility,'" Dr. Harish Hande says. "I think I should be socially responsible in the first place. Why should I create those words as if social responsibility is something else? You are a corporation, and you should feel socially responsible. So why create a separate category with all these terms?"

Henry Mintzberg adds, "Business as currently constituted, and as it currently behaves, isn't solving the problem. I don't care how green Walmart gets. Walmart might save lots of paper and other things, but there's so much exploitation going on. I applaud corporate social responsibility. We need as much of it as we can get. But if anybody thinks that corporate social responsibility is going to make up for corporate social irresponsibility, then they've got their head in the sand."

Wilson suggests "changing the words 'corporate social responsibility' to 'corporate social *opportunity*,' because with opportunity comes excitement and enthusiasm. With responsibility, there's a sense of obligation and lethargy. Corporate social opportunity involves thinking about investments differently. So many people think of it as going through the income statement. I think of it as going through the balance sheet. The balance sheet includes changing the world. The world's worth more when you give money to it. You've made the world better. It's an asset on your balance sheet. That's the new conversation to be had. Take some of your financial capital, apply your intellectual capital, and change the world."

Mintzberg adds his weight to the argument about where the change must come from. "It's going to be social issues on the part of regular people; it's not going to be government, and it's not going to be business. Government is too co-opted, too much in bed with some of the worst forces of business."

Mintzberg adds that "even decent business can't solve the problem when there's so much indecency going on." In other words, business as it currently is in its unawakened state cannot make the difference that's needed, even if it behaves more responsibly from time to time. Far more is required, involving nothing less than a transformation of the business world. For all the enthusiasm of those who seek to make a difference through business, Mintzberg is correct that the current model simply cannot cut the mustard.

However, what would happen were companies everywhere to awaken? What if they were to realize how dependent they are on communities, and how much they need to be supportive of both private and government enterprise? What if they were to allow communities to take the lead, as opposed to arrogantly swooping in to reshape communities in line with *their* particular vision? Were companies awakened, the power they could wield on behalf of humanity would enable not only communities, but whole countries, to help themselves.

Sadly—and indeed tragically—as business has grown in power, its ties to government have deepened. This has drowned out the voices of ordinary citizens, and at times even whole communities. Many people have concluded, often cynically, that business now runs many governments. The implication of this is that without the involvement of business in global problem-solving, nothing of substance will come from governments.

This point is fleshed out in Mintzberg's online pamphlet Rebalancing Society, in which he writes, "We have to leave behind the linear politics of left, right, and center, to understand that a balanced society, like a stable stool, has to rest on three solid legs: a public sector of political forces rooted in respected governments, a private sector of economic forces based on responsible businesses, and a plural sector of social forces manifested in robust communities."[2]

The means to this is neither socialism nor capitalism, but awareness. An awakened planet requires an awakened economy, and an awakened economy will need all of us to shift our consciousness from "me" to "we." This shift will involve a reprioritizing of our barometer of success from "profit for profit's sake" to *meaning* and *wisdom*.

The Problem Begins at Home

For an awakened economy to develop apace, it will be necessary for the shift that's getting underway in companies to be reflected in what's taught in business schools, but even before that, at home.

Says Renewal Funds' Joel Solomon, "Business has basically been designed as war." He cites how this shows up in the language we often associate with business: win, number one, beat, compete, outsmart, gain dominance, monopoly, biggest. The basic philosophy of so many in business is "if it's not illegal and it improves my financial bottom line, I have a responsibility to do it." Solomon comments, "I think that's corrupt."

This mentality goes even further, as Solomon explains: "If it is illegal, and if I'm powerful enough, I can influence, bribe, cajole, and bully the people who write the laws to change the law so that it becomes legal. So we've normalized war and violence and domination in our economic model, and therefore our workplace."

A large part of the problem is a failure to distinguish between profit maximization and financial sustainability. As Dr. Hande expresses it, "Unfortunately, younger minds in our country have begun to believe that business has to be ruthless and corrupt." He cites an "overarching emphasis on excel-sheet planning" in most of the top business schools, "leading young business minds to concentrate solely on profit maximization. Let me caution—profit maximization and financial sustainability are two completely different things. In the business world, we have conveniently merged them together."[3]

Henry Mintzberg points out additional problems. "I think the whole mindset of MBA programs is absolutely dysfunctional. It starts with a premise that's not only false but also hubristic—the idea that you can create managers in the classroom. It's absolutely not true. But by training people out of context, these schools are essentially creating mercenaries, people who think they can run anything. And that's the problem—it's not the solution."

Mintzberg advises, "The first thing business schools can do is to end the lie that they're training managers. At least this would reduce the hubris. They are training people to go into financial analysis and marketing research, so they need to stop claiming that these individuals are going to be leading the world."

Mintzberg relates how Michael Jensen, who taught the most popular elective course at Harvard for years, wrote an article in which he quoted the story of George Bernard Shaw saying to a famous actress aboard a ship, "Would you sleep with me for $1 million?" She responded that she would. Then Shaw suggested, "How about for $10?" To which the actress retorted, "What do you think I am?" Shaw replied, "We've established that. Now we're just haggling about the price."

The problem is that at Harvard a story like this was followed up with the statement, "Like it or not, everybody has their price." In other words, we're all whores in business. So why are we surprised when a scandal like Enron erupts or we read about the financial improprieties of JPMorgan Chase and Goldman Sachs?

In an article in the online India edition of *Forbes* magazine, Dr. Hande comments on how we always hear from the business world that there's a need to increase the value for shareholders. "This is a very lopsided statement," Hande insists, suggesting that what businesses should really work toward is to increase the value for *all* stakeholders, which includes end-users, employees, management, and shareholders.[4]

Mintzberg stresses that the shift in attitudes needs to extend beyond a company's employees to the wider community. Hande goes on to say, "It's a total shift in attitudes really. It's a shift not only concerning people working for the company, but a shift that's about customers. It's about not having people be exploited for every last cent or bamboozled by pricing that nobody can understand because there's a few bucks to be made. It's about customers who are valued. Similarly with suppliers, who need to be treated decently because it's not a question of squeezing money out of them for the next year. It's a matter of having sustainable relationships."[5]

12

WHAT MAKES AN EXECUTIVE "AWAKENED"?

Have you at some point been in a situation in which a leader captured your heart, mind, and soul to the point you were moved to action? If so, did you happen to reflect on what it was about this individual that so captivated you?

The ability to captivate someone like this isn't exactly a skill set, although skill is definitely a part of it. Rather, it has to do with the *quality* of the person themselves. There's something about their manner of being that draws us to them and commands our attention. This quality is often referred to as a sense of "presence." Certain individuals exude a strong sense of presence.

Let's be clear that we aren't talking about people with big egos or charismatic types who may be sociopaths. Some of these individuals can impress and charm, and may have the ability to captivate individuals in the same way as someone with a strong sense of presence. However, in these cases the ability to inspire tends to soon wear off.

Presence is an energy, transmitted almost like light— unseen, and yet capable of revealing everything it touches. Consequently, when we are around a person with great presence, we experience a palpable feeling of our interconnectedness. There's a realness about the encounter, and both giver and receiver are bound by the authenticity and sheer honesty of the connection.

The feeling of presence we experience in such individuals conveys the idea they are "coming from the right place." Consequently, there's a sense in which an awakened executive doesn't have to lead in the usual way we might think of leading others. Rather, as a natural byproduct of the vision awakened leaders are in the process of manifesting within themselves, we are inspired to become more than we so far know ourselves to be. Simply by means of their very being, they create the space for us to be led by our own true nature.

One of the main reasons an awakened executive's vision not only excites us, but actually feels attainable, is that we experience in them a combination of enthusiasm and practicality. We are captured not only by their genius, but also their groundedness. Firmly present in the reality of the moment, they embody the feeling of prosperity, satisfaction, and harmony to which they seek to lead the rest of us. It's as if by exemplifying what we desire for ourselves, they elevate something in all of us.

At its best, then, effective leadership is a dance between, on the one side, inspiration, motivation, intellectual challenge, and the ability to influence others, and on the other side the everyday execution of multiple roles and responsibilities. Because this dance flows from presence, it's both graceful and serene. For these reasons, leading from presence is devoid of the desperate role juggling we encounter among egos in so much of the business world. Since an awakened executive is simply being themselves, they exude a deep calm that's powerful in itself, without any need for the added "show" of ego.

It's because the awakened executive's energy seems almost to emanate from beyond themselves, even as their vision soars well beyond most people's limited view, that such an individual is more easily able to engage us in their enterprise. We sense they are coming from a place that's going to benefit us and others.

The Importance of Spaciousness for Guidance

Life has a way of throwing us curves, and the business world with its volatility is certainly no exception. When it comes to dealing with unexpected circumstances, awakened executives certainly know how to scenario plan. Using current data and incorporating various human and systemic factors, they analyze and simulate an array of possible scenarios. They know the importance of contingency planning because they realize the future is unpredictable.

Awakened executives are attuned to threats and changes in their environment, but channel fear and worry into action. Such individuals have the ability to recognize paradox and can entertain opposing thoughts without stress or confusion, and even strategically embody polarities—bold or passive, leader or follower. They know in the moment when to bring out which type of energy—leading when leadership is called for, sitting back to listen when sitting back is called for, and pitching in as part of the team when necessary. Ensuring that all the different elements at play work in an integrated fashion toward a purpose that's beyond any of our individual intentions, awakened executives are able to see what role needs to be played in a situation to make that situation work. Their down-to-earth approachability also aids in their ability to align personal motivation and goals with collective or organizational goals.

Awakened executives are adaptable and don't come from a fixed position. They recognize that the more our attention is captured by compulsive thinking and reacting, the more we tend to resist the reality of the moment, telling ourselves that "such and such shouldn't be happening" and "this isn't how we planned things."

When we resist the present moment, instead of allowing it to be what it is, we miss the hidden opportunities it contains. With an awakened executive, the usual inner talk we associate with thinking, and the resistance it generates, quiets down substantially. As this happens, we notice a kind of spacious quietness within us.

A big part of what brings about this spaciousness is a willingness to surrender to life as it is. Generally, "surrender" isn't a word we associate with business and leadership. However, we need to understand it in a particular way. In the body, surrender and acceptance are reflected in unclenched muscles and the ability to rest in the feeling of an expanded heart. With heart open and the body at ease, we can more easily notice the vibrant stillness at our center—a stillness usually obscured by an agitated mind and body.

A sure indication we are awakening as an executive is a greater degree of trust in the innate wisdom of life to guide our business. While we may receive a powerful vision for our work that flows from an inner sense of spaciousness, we also receive practical answers to unexpected situations that arise, of which there are many in the business world. Entering into the stillness of the heart, we listen deeply for what's required in the moment. Being alert, with little internal chatter, and possessing a sense of wonder makes us agile learners. Not fixated on goals, we are open and naturally curious. Instead of being attached to a particular outcome, we are interested in learning and experiencing life.

Spaciousness, and the stillness that accompanies it, is an aspect of the unknown, the mysterious formlessness from which all people, objects, and energy arise. If you have learned to observe your inner life, you may have noticed that many of your best ideas and impulses arise out of this mysterious spaciousness within. Thus, entering into spaciousness really is entering the unknown. Awakened executives are keenly aware that no one can predict what will happen in the future, but they are willing to take thoughtful risks with hopes of creating a positive future for all.

This devoted, focused attentiveness contains a practical intelligence about how to make things work and how to sustain operations. This includes being financially prudent and realistic about what resources are available and how we work with those resources. This sensibility is as powerful for groups as it is for individuals. All together, this produces a discipline that makes organizations hum like a fine-tuned machine.

Executives who exude this trait of the intentional pause give other people permission to pause, as well. When we turn down the frenetic energy at key moments, we keep our employees balanced, which brings out their best work.

By fostering an atmosphere of spaciousness in the company's personnel, we not only make tasks so much more enjoyable than when they are performed under the constant pressure that mars so many work environments, but we also actually encourage creativity.

For this reason, as well as working on themselves, awakened executives allow their people room to work on themselves also. In line with this, there's an appreciation for silence in the company as a whole—a valuing of appropriate non-doing. This non-doing has nothing in common with being lazy or disengaged, but has more to do with not filling up all the creative space with chatter. This allows something unexpected to emerge from the space that lies between our fears and our desires.

In other words, awakened executives aren't afraid of a break in the action in their organization. In fact, it's crucial that "full steam ahead" is tempered with the ability to pause. We're not talking about a pause to just daydream. Rather, the purpose is to breathe and take stock of where we are. We disengage from the momentum in order to become more grounded in our approach to the task at hand. Whatever work you are doing—on the computer or smart phone—stop for a minute, breathe, and feel your body. If you are sitting for long periods, stand up and move.

I believe that the ability to engage in this kind of non-doing is especially needed in today's workplaces, for it facilitates being highly alert and simultaneously at ease. When we come from this balance, we are likely to be so stimulated by and interested in what engages us that our efforts feel almost effortless—as if we were practically "doing nothing." So absorbed are we, so caught up in the flow of our work, that we even lose track of time.

Develop the Art of "Holding the Space"

Have you ever stopped to consider how many times you are surprised by something in your day?

Although we are all aware of being surprised at times, we often fail to capitalize on the potential that surprise holds. Marching relentlessly through our daily routine, we miss magnificent opportunities because we don't nurture within ourselves the feeling of *availability*. Not only availability to what's happening around us, but also to fresh ideas that may be trying to arise within us.

To hold the space for something new to emerge requires us to let go of our attachment to a certain outcome to situations. While this can cause us to feel exposed, there's nothing negative about it, even though many of us have been conditioned to think of slowing a project's progress as negative. Letting go of our attachment to a particular outcome means we are less closed off and therefore more available for new inspiration, connection, and creativity. It helps to be aware that new things often feel more fragile, even as a sapling is far less solid than the thick trunk of an established oak. Yet just as the survival of the forest depends on saplings, we need to nurture the tentative insights and new opportunities that come our way, giving them space to breathe.

Rushing a product to market can be a costly mistake, both in terms of customers and also the effect on the company's personnel. Impatience results in a pressured working atmosphere that spawns errors, tension, and dissatisfaction, robbing everyone of the enjoyment of work. Awakened executives know when it's right to actively push something through, but also when it's wisest to put space around a project that's begun to feel cumbersome. They discern when, like a good wine, a project needs time to breathe. They trust that by giving the project the space to breathe, insight and clarity will emerge.

When we accept that things take as long as they take, we free ourselves to put our patient attention into every part of the process to ensure what comes out is superlative. By allowing projects to unfold in the space they deserve, we don't overextend ourselves, which enables us to preserve our enthusiasm and creative energy for each stage of the process. In this way, we avoid the pitfall of becoming depleted and having to resort to fancy footwork to sell what we truly haven't prepared for.

The field of spacious presence generated between colleagues is an important source of creativity and innovation. Tuning into and aligning with this field gives us access to what artists, designers, and geniuses of all kinds have accessed throughout the ages. The same life intelligence that has assembled bodies, brains, planets, and the universe itself can flow into our thoughts and lead us to innovative breakthroughs. The awareness that cultivates presence is, thus, the skill that enhances all other skills.

13

THE DIFFERENCE AN
AWAKENED EXECUTIVE MAKES

Awakened leaders challenge, inspire, and persuade the people they work with by articulating meaning and furnishing an understanding of whatever action is required. Such individuals "know what they are about" more than most do.

These executives focus on unrestrained fact-finding so that the truth of a situation can emerge. Curiosity, openness, and a willingness to keep investigating and uncovering information are crucial to this process. Awakened executives get to the bottom of things, however brutal the reality may be. They then develop a clear set of priorities for the team to focus on.

An effective executive has to be willing to put themselves at risk by saying what needs to be said. The fact they can be both highly sensitive and brutally honest as need demands allows for a *realness* to emerge in an organization. When a leader is authentic in this way, it tends to be empowering for everybody.

This is congruent with the insight of Lynne Twist, the creator of the Hunger Project and author of *The Soul of Money*, who draws an important distinction between taking a position and taking a stand. When we take a position, it's usually against something, which generates opposition. When we take a stand, something special happens. It invites people on all sides to stand with us in the challenge, whatever it may be. Whereas positions may divide us, taking a stand generates trust, is life affirming, and can unite us. Since a stand comes from our heart and manifests as a powerful sense of presence, often a situation shifts profoundly. Our varied positions begin to dissolve as we recognize that what we are doing isn't working, opening the way for us to find another way forward together.[1]

Think of someone who is willing to take a stand, but never a position against others. The energy of their presence, coupled with courageous conviction, can draw people in and inspire them to work together to transform a system that appears immoveable

How to Avoid Taking the Wrong Stand

The downside to this is that an executive can sometimes take a stand that's the wrong strategy. A strong will, firm conviction, but flawed vision can spiral down into belligerence, insistence, and expediency. Instead of being affected by the truth of the moment, the executive is driven by a fearful and domineering ego. In such a situation, the company may experience severe disruption—and in some cases not survive. More than one CEO has driven a formerly thriving business into the ground.

If you are an executive, how can you tell whether you are taking a stand that arises from awareness or from either flawed information or your ego?

When executives take a stand that doesn't truly arise from

awareness, they tend to display the kind of impatience discussed toward the end of the last chapter—a rushed feeling that's counterproductive to the creative process. Caught up in the enthusiasm they are trying to generate, there's no valuing of the "cooking process." Wanting to get to the good stuff at the end, they fail to allow for sufficient preparation, often jumping on the first ideas that emerge instead of examining whether they are the best the team could come up with.

If you are an executive, to avoid becoming unbalanced in this way, watch for a tendency to express a false expertise in an attempt to push an agenda through. If you haven't done your homework, you don't really know what you are talking about. To cover up your lack of information, you may then resort to project-related jargon that sounds good but isn't based on solid ground. Presenting such flawed information in an exciting package may well get the energy going, which allows the company to pretend they are headed somewhere exciting despite an absence of vital details. For a time, a whole organization can operate this way, pretty much flying by the seat of its pants—though anyone observant enough will realize a crash is all but inevitable.

Strategic passion gives executives not only the courage to take a stand, but the wisdom to examine their decisions in the light of their clear values, coupled with a willingness to consult their team in the setting of goals and schedules. In this way, they ensure the stand they take emerges from their best and wisest self. We need commitment and passion for sure. But without a well-tempered wisdom and real knowledge of the tasks we are undertaking, passion can rapidly head us off course. Head and heart need to work together. When we have this inner congruence, people notice.

The degree of integrity with which executives interact with others on the team determines the degree to which they are ultimately admired, respected, and trusted. When they demonstrate a high standard of ethical and moral conduct, people know they can be relied on to do the right thing. Such leaders function as signposts of hope, which leads to being emulated by their employees, whose commitment to the organization is strong because, with this kind of leadership, it happens at the heart level.

Let Values Be Your Compass

When it comes to leading effectively, Mark Montemurro, Vice President at Baytex Energy, says, "It's really crucial to sit back and examine what's important, what your values are, and to bring that presence to the workplace."

BluEarth Renewables' Kent Brown agrees, commenting, "Values are everything."

A good example of a company that lives its values is the organization Canadian Hydro Developers. Over a twenty-year period, they did exactly what they said they would, consistently providing renewable energy. They treated the earth with respect, when with their skill sets and experience they probably could have made a lot more money building an oil and gas company.

When executives and employees get honest with themselves, this reflects in their marketing techniques. Can a company be awakened if it uses marketing and ad techniques that, instead of reflecting high values, are designed to manipulate the public?

When my sons were watching the Sochi Olympics, I was shocked to witness a McDonalds ad correlating a chicken

McNugget to a gold medal. In the world of advertising, we see everything from "soft drinks equal happiness" to countless portrayals of women as objects. As for words like "natural," which these days are bandied about to sell all kinds of foodstuffs, in so many cases they have no more real value than making a statement such as "arsenic is 'natural.'" Some companies have even watered down the term "organic" to such an extent as to be all but meaningless. Certainly such terms often fail to convey the image the public has of what's intended. It's good to remember that even though such techniques may offer a certain expediency in marketing, the public eventually does find out.

In a landscape of many competing ads, sometimes there's a fine line between dishonest manipulation and capturing a potential buyer's attention. For this reason, each company needs to ask itself how honest it is in how it presents itself from the point of view of the four Ps: product, placement, promotion, and price. Are we giving people the real deal, or something considerably less value-oriented?

As awareness is cultivated in many more companies, hopefully we will have to endure less and less manipulation and exploitation. Each of us can accelerate the shift toward honest marketing by simply saying "no thank you" to those companies that attempt to manipulate us.

On a different front, can a company be called awakened if it encourages the local chamber of commerce to lobby government at all levels, while also funding political campaigns that favor deregulation and cutting social services? And what about the heavy funding and lobbying to shift the tax burden and environmental impact from itself to the surrounding community that sustains it? In the process of awakening, companies have to take a hard look at their practices, searching every crevice for uncaring, greedy behavior.

When an executive identifies an area in which the company doesn't have to settle for "business as usual" just because it's the way it has always operated, personnel are inspired to believe they are capable of responding to something higher and deeper in themselves. Because they can identify with the leader's values and the organization's purpose, it makes it easier for them to support the vision.

It's vital we continually examine our values and also invite ongoing scrutiny on the part of those we work with. If the ego gets a hold of our values, our higher sensibility can quickly be reduced to a fixed notion of how people and situations are supposed to be. Then, instead of *inviting* personnel to take a stand with us, we operate from inflexibility, demanding loyalty. As our level of awareness and sense of connectedness drops, having silenced the rigorous questioning we so need, we lose the ability to distinguish between our personal agenda and what's needed objectively. We convince ourselves we are operating from an altruistic and moral perspective, when in fact the ego has slipped in to defend our position. The fact we've stopped listening can frustrate and alienate others on the team, who now feel they are neither being seen nor heard.

To be uncompromising can be a cherished quality unless we lose perspective and our heart begins to close. Then our high values can devolve into obsessing over trivial matters and thus create a judgmental and obstructionist atmosphere. For this reason, all of us need to ask ourselves, "Am I uncompromisingly taking a virtuous stand, or am I getting bogged down in minutiae by trying to control a process, thereby sabotaging group synergy?"

Deep values require a deep awareness of ourselves that includes the input of our peers. The deeper we go, the more we realize we are all connected and rely on each other for our survival and happiness. It's this connectedness, which fuels a desire to benefit each other, that's the driving force of our values.

Ways to Activate Your Moral Spine

Taking a "stand" isn't just metaphorical. It has a kinesthetic element, which is why we refer to certain individuals as lacking "spine."

Anything that makes us more aware of our spine helps us to activate our ability to take a stand. Something about feeling our backbone and being aware of its verticality enables us to feel more plugged into a deep inner wisdom. We feel more aligned, relaxed, and supported by life. A natural sense of self-respect and dignity emerges. To the degree this comes across to people, they sense we recognize and honor their dignity too.

We can keep our spine feeling relaxed and flowing by stretching and relaxing body parts, engaging in yoga, and by sitting upright and walking upright as if suspended from a wire attached to the top of the head. In all these contexts, it's helpful to place attention on feeling our spine.

Having stressed the key role values play, it's necessary to be aware that becoming overtly serious and rigidly attached to values can have a negative kinesthetic effect. If we allow ourselves to build a story around a particular value, or perhaps see ourselves as one of the few people with values in a world that's suffering terribly as a result of a lack of values, we can become heavy, grim, and resentful—emotional states that all manifest in the body, showing in such things as our countenance, posture, and gait.

Genuine upset and sadness have their place, but we need to distinguish such natural responses to loss, for instance, from when they arise as part of an old, oft-repeated, burdensome story. The antidote is to be fully present in whatever we are engaged in, which enables us to feel in a manner and to a degree that's appropriate to the situation. In this way we guard against becoming caught up in thoughts and emotions generated by the stories we tell ourselves about how awful things are.

Now that we've pointed out some of the potential pitfalls of taking a stand, how can we counter these? There are a number of traditional techniques that can be useful. As we have seen, working with the body and with sensation is an efficient way to move through stuck attitudes and emotions, so I will present a couple of techniques from the yogic tradition. One of these is a balancing technique known in Sanskrit as *uttanasana*. This is a pose that takes the form of a bodily forward fold. The term means "intense and deliberate." It's purpose is to soothe the nervous system.

If you feel yourself becoming belligerent or fixated on a particular course, provided you are physically able, are healthy, and don't have back problems, stand with your feet together and soles grounded. Hinge forward from the hips, letting the head and arms hang loose or holding your elbows. This isn't about touching your toes, but about the moments in between. Take eight deep breaths in this position as an aid to placing space around the situation and allowing yourself to return to a balanced state.

The Practicalities of Being an Executive

Awakened leaders build everyone up and see every situation as an ally—a potential teacher and guide.

This being the case, what happens when a leader with exceptional coaching skills grooms someone on their team to be stronger than themselves? Can such a leader see the individual they have trained as an ally, or do they begin to regard the person as a rival?

An awakened executive is able to "see the stardust"—the elements in ourselves that are truly amazing—in both themselves *and* others, no matter what the circumstances.[2] They see the energy that unites all of us in every eyeball. This is what makes them not only an effective coach of high performance, but also an effective manager of such performance.

Being challenged by rising talent can be viewed either as threatening or something to capitalize on. Even though at times it may seem diversity and harmony can't coexist in a business environment, requiring one to be sacrificed for the other, the awakened executive appreciates that both are in fact required if the company is to go beyond the mediocre and excel. Such an executive can hold the paradox because they understand that tending to and cultivating these two energies is worth the effort. Sensing when one aspect needs to be emphasized more than the other, they maintain an inclusive approach. Any potential discord is enveloped in tolerance, acceptance, and peace.

To take this a step further, since it's such an important aspect of being a leader, awakened executives value contrasting opinions because they understand that, to get at the truth, a company needs both diversity and harmony. Such executives realize it's possible to hold in mind two opposing hypotheses, using them to allow the real truth to emerge, then act on that deeper truth. Don't mistake this for regression toward the mean, but rather see it as a new way of creating.

Promoting harmony also requires acknowledging people for how they have contributed, and sometimes for simply being present throughout the process.

The more we know how to find harmony within ourselves, the easier it will be to promote it with our colleagues and employees. Again, there are many traditional techniques that can be enormously helpful in this regard. For example, classic meditation can teach us to find harmony within discord. We learn to be the eye of the storm—at ease, while aware of the risks around us and alert to what needs to be done. Yoga or tai chi can help us find balance. A yoga pose is the epitome of learning to be comfortable in an uncomfortable position.

When leaders find a soothing way of approaching problems that's distinct from an adrenalized motivational approach, employees often in due course find themselves mirroring their leader's reasonableness. They then tend to do better work because they feel internally grounded, relaxed, and opened up. Without this grounded openness, it can be difficult to develop a creative team.

Truth, love, wisdom, peace, and a sense of fulfillment are a natural part of our developed nature, whereas the under-developed human, locked in ego, not only perceives nearly everyone as a potential threat but always wants more and is never satisfied. In this less developed state, we rely on prim-itive cleverness to manipulate and survive. Due to perceiv-ing all of us as separate, disconnected, and unrelated, fear reigns—the kind of fear that drives so much of our present bipolar economy.

14

BEYOND ROLES

"By examining employee turnover records for individual stores," the Harvard Business Review reports, "Taco Bell has discovered that the 20% of stores with the lowest turnover rates enjoy double the sales and 55% higher profits than the 20% of stores with the highest employee turnover rates."[1] In the light of this, we might ask what's responsible for employee turnover rates.

According to Buckingham and Coffman,[2] how long employees stay, and how productive they are while they are with a company, is determined by the relationship with their immediate supervisor. People leave the one to whom they report directly far more than they leave companies, per se.

The most disengaged group of workers are those with a manager who simply isn't paying attention. In such a case, there's a 40% chance workers will be disengaged, if not filled with hostility. However, when a manager focuses on the strengths of individuals, the chance of those people being disengaged is a mere 1%.[3]

If you have a turnover problem, take a look at the reporting relationship. What sorts of reports are you getting? Do you have the sense that managers actually know the people they work with and the quality of their work? One of the signs of a great manager is the ability to describe the talents, thinking, and relationship style of their direct reports.

It's important to be clear that management and leadership aren't necessarily the same thing. In any organization, leaders set the tone, creating a culture. Managers execute, often by the book, enacting the process set by the leadership. Some of us make extremely good managers, whereas others of us make strong leaders. Both are needed, although management without leadership can tend to infuse a business with a rote feeling, whereas leadership without management can be chaos.

Writing in *Money*, Tony Robbins comments, "To the question, 'What is leadership? How do you define it?' Mary Callahan Erdoes responds: 'It's important not to confuse management with leadership. For me, leadership means not asking anyone to do anything I wouldn't do myself. It's waking up every morning trying to make your organization a better place. I truly believe that I work for the people of J.P. Morgan Asset Management, not the other way around, and because of that, I try to see beyond what people even see themselves.'"[4] Callahan Erdoes has been called Wall Street's Trillion Dollar Woman and is CEO, J.P. Morgan Asset Management Division.

Callahan Erdoes adds: "Having been a portfolio manager, client advisor, and business leader, I know what we're capable of achieving for our clients. So I consider it my job not just to lead our teams but to get in the trenches alongside them and join them on the journey."[5]

An outstanding leader today is really a coach. Their task is to be a facilitator of other people's potential and to help set the field for success. Excellent companies survive with excellent leadership coupled with effective management. There are countless individuals in management who know nothing of the kind of humanizing management style we are talking about. A major reason some of the big-name companies go down the drain is that they are driven into the ground by a management technician who is presumed to be a leader but has little grasp of what leadership entails. We need managers who can implement at different levels, but a leader can't be only a technician in this way.

In this chapter, our focus will be on some of the skills that make for both good management and effective leadership.

Management and Leadership Require the Ability to Relate

When we analyzed the instincts of business managers, leaders, and executives, the blind spot for the sample was "magnetic" relationships, the ability to go deep with one another. If going deep is a blind spot of our leaders, this will surely affect us organizationally.

An authentic relationship isn't dominated by people's egos, which involve posturing and putting on an act. Rather, such a relationship is built on genuine connection in which neither is making demands of the other, neither placing expectations on the other to be somehow different from their real self. There is simply a "being with" one another, which is the only way a relationship can be meaningful.

Many managers don't take time to develop meaningful relationships in which they are truly present with their staff because they fail to recognize the crucial role these individuals play in a business. They think of people as disposable, easily replaced, and are oblivious of the high cost such an approach carries with it.

Have you ever considered that, without relationships, nothing would exist? As internationally renowned Buddhist teacher Thich Nhat Hanh states, "We have no need of a separate self or a separate existence. In fact, nothing can exist by itself. We must inter-be with all things. Look at a flower. It cannot exist by itself. It can only inter-be with the whole cosmos. And that is true for you, too."[6] Even if you lead an isolated life on a mountaintop, you exist in relation to the mountain, the climate, and nature all around you. If someone enters your thoughts, although their body may not be present, you are still mentally and emotionally engaged with them, and thus they can affect you from far away.

However we choose to live, our relationships are a key element of a life that's meaningful. One reason for this is that they are where we can learn a great deal about ourselves. In the mirror we call the "other," we have an opportunity to discover what we might never otherwise discern about ourselves. Awakened managers, along with awakened teams, recognize the importance of seeing themselves in the other. They are also conscious of the need to quiet their mind so that their judgments and reactions don't clutter the view.

In its highest form, a relationship is much more than a structure of familiar habits and expectations. Rather, it's a spontaneously felt awareness that's always fresh, always emerging, and capable of producing a synergy greater than its individual components. Such awareness enables us to look beyond the old hurts and assumptions we have of each other and to see each other afresh, which is crucial if a company is to draw each individual's potential out and thereby take maximum advantage of its pool of talent.

The traditional hierarchical arrangement in workplaces

no longer serves us well. Everyone needs to be regarded as a human being with dignity. Now, more than ever, it's important that even the lowliest individuals in a company should never be treated as if they were a dime a dozen. Why should a manager care about them? Florian Heiner, General Manager of a hotel in a large upscale chain, gives the reason: "Because everyone in your company, together with your customers, will judge your product as genuine when they see how you treat those who fulfill the most menial of tasks. Remember, from the top down to the very bottom, you are creating a culture. This culture is either one of excellence, which is built on faith in your employees, or one of fear, which will drag not only individual employees down but ultimately the whole company. Happy workers coupled with a worthwhile product are the keys to success in any venture. Good management recognizes the importance of making the entire workday a happy experience. People need to look forward to coming to work."[7]

Management needs to recognize that when people love their work, they are also healthier and hence rarely absent. One of the keys to achieving such an atmosphere is that we don't stretch our staff to the point they become resentful, which then reverberates in less robust health and a sullen attitude toward the public. As we saw in an earlier chapter, we have to be conscious of their needs—not just at work, but in the whole of their life.

Relationships and Relatedness

Being a colleague is a structure, being a parent is a structure, and being a couple is a structure. By "structure," I'm referring to defined roles. These tend to be quite traditional.

For instance, parents tend to see themselves as being there to teach their children. In a traditional business hierarchy, there tend to be people we are more or less able to speak to depending on their rank. People can be in such structures and be quite disconnected.

Beyond the structure of a relationship lies the possibility of real connection, which involves an awareness of the field of *us*. This is unique with any two people. If you have three or four, there's going to be a unique field consisting of those three or four. When there's connection, the parties feel devotion to themselves, to the other, and to what's happening that involves them in a synergy.

You can see the difference between the structure of relationships and a more felt sense of relating in how we wave to one another in the hallway or perhaps say, "Hi, how are you?" as we pat each other on the back. It may be harmless or even pleasant, yet it's a conditioned response; there's no real experience of one another in either the question or the response. The more structure we establish, the more it tends to deprive us of actually relating, which is the sense of being with each other. The result is that, lost in a maze of patterns, we behave toward one another based on fear rather than real connection.

When something isn't working relationally, the solution isn't only to add more structure to the relationship. What's really required is to take each other in more directly, letting ourselves be seen and known as we really are. This is more than just letting our opinions be known. It involves openness and availability. The ability to be present and grounded allows us to experience real engagement. When leaders feel grounded and can be truly present, it gives them the strength to open themselves up, as well as to address grievances, hurt, and disappointment in both themselves and others creatively. There's much less need for drama because people feel seen and heard.

Relatedness is such an important aspect of human cooperation, and yet many of us don't seem to know how to achieve it. However, with the explosion of social media, the importance of relatedness is returning to many modern, progressive societies where, by and large, it has diminished. Social media are helping people awaken to the element of themselves that longs to relate. The popularity of such media is an expression of how desperate people are to find some quality of relatedness. Of course, just because two people connect via social media doesn't necessarily mean they are relating more, only that social media is shedding light on their need and desire to relate.

In many developing countries, where there is often a lack of basics such as money or even food, what people do often have is each other. Relatedness on a social level is what in South Africa they call "ubuntu," which was a central theme for Nelson Mandela and his vision of leadership. It isn't merely belonging, although this is one element of it. It's a sense of personal connection and belonging. Ubuntu is "the belief in a universal bond of sharing that connects all humanity."[8]

People in awakened relationships are profoundly aware of how connected they are to each other. Better together than they are apart, they realize they are able to see and understand the world more fully as a result of their different outlooks, skills, and interests. The relationship creates a relaxed, supportive atmosphere in which to discover each other's personality traits and gifts. Sharing from our strengths, while minimizing each other's weaknesses, is extremely beneficial because it maximizes our accomplishments. When this happens, we intuitively know that relatedness is what our heart has been longing for—that it's what we're really seeking from relationships, be they professional or personal.

Unlike relationships as primary structures, in relatedness there's less in the way of an *idea* about ourselves and more direct *experience* of ourselves. There's also less idea about the other and more direct experience of the other. This experience of self and other is how authentic relatedness develops. A relationship can only truly be called "awakened" if there's a consistent element of relatedness in it. It's also a way of noticing how present we are, since if we aren't enjoying a measure of relatedness, we aren't really present—and only when we are present do we create, function, and produce at an optimal level.

This is where many self-described "spiritual" folk make a mistake. They may be sitting there trying to hold onto some presence-like experience, as they imagine distracting actions on the part of others are hampering their ability to be present. However, presence has nothing to do with being in a deep trance-like state and not really with those around us. If we want to be in the field of relatedness, we need to relate to what others are doing.

Spaciousness in Relationships

In awakened relationships, people are also autonomous in the sense that they aren't in each other's space. They know how to be independent, and they give each other space as needed. This is especially important for managers to bear in mind. Giving someone space implies a respect for the person.

The consequence of such respect is that individuals don't try to change one another. Neither do they either belittle or aggrandize the other person, as so often happens between team members. Instead, acceptance of each other breeds mutual respect and a desire to be open about our hopes, abilities, limitations, and concerns. It's from such openness that truly productive interaction arises.

Whenever there's a problem, if individuals feel compassionately seen and heard by one another, this functions as a balm. The result is that even though the problem may still be present, any reactivity subsides. Then the team can address the problem from a place of groundedness, which tends to bring clarity. With practice, we are more able to show up and be there completely with someone even when that person is lost in thought and emotional reactivity. We don't have to wait for others to be present in order to be present with them. This, in a very real and practical sense, is one of the advantages of awakened leadership. We initiate presence and support, instead of waiting for others to do it for us. This is the true meaning of support, and it comes from feeling supported by life itself.

To be able to be there for each other is qualitatively different from propping up a weak link, and awakened companies exude consistent reciprocal support. Personnel come to work because they enjoy interacting with the people working there, a consequence of which is that they naturally support one another when such is temporarily needed. People in the company almost feel like they will be caught before they fall. They have the sense that someone "has their back." This safe, supportive space encourages the pursuit of self-awareness and self-improvement, factors that make employees better at their jobs.

Genuine leadership and management is in large measure the quality of listening deeply. This involves checking in with ourselves for what feels true for us, then checking in with the other person. The awakened person is able to connect to something deeper within themselves that's beyond mere beliefs and reactions. This gives them the ability to look beyond the beliefs and reactions of those they are managing, instead seeing something deeper in each individual. Employees sense their manager isn't just "phoning it in," pretending to care when really they want to move on to their own agenda.

A disengaged manager is likely to mistakenly see the other as a problem to be fixed. They will be in a hurry to neutralize what they perceive as a threat to their own stability and a group's dynamics. In contrast, an engaged manager is able to fully engage an employee who either disengages or reacts strongly because they feel abused, unappreciated, or that their opinions go unacknowledged. Such a manager can hold the space for all possibilities, including the employee's reactivity and resistance to what's taking place. The manager might say, "I feel this isn't working for you, but that we've in some way crossed a line with you. Tell me about that, and also how we might enable you to feel a part of the conversation. Is there a way we can repair things to make you feel valued, respected, and heard as you deserve to be?" Feeling seen and heard, the employee's reactivity begins to dissipate.

Allowing for spaciousness to emerge during the expression of strong emotions doesn't mean we let others walk all over us. While we want to be open to whatever emerges, unnecessary critique, incessant analysis, and excessive reactivity can collapse the shared field of presence. When we are grounded, we don't let others push us around with their agendas or emotions.

If a person's reactions are too disruptive or accompanied by unrealistic demands, we utter a firm yet gentle "no"—or what the Buddha referred to as a "noble no."

Instead of allowing someone's ego to manipulate and disrupt other employees to a point of group fragmentation, an engaged manager can reassure the person this is just the beginning, and we will find a solution together. We also inform them that it would be best to pursue this in private. Without any judgment, the awakened person meets the other in a feeling state that's more fundamental than their defenses.

When team members find out they can be angry in a situation and still be honored, it doesn't encourage them to be angry again. It lets them know their voice will be heard, which means they have less incentive to express themselves in a dysfunctional manner in the future.

In these and other ways, as colleagues, we grow in our support of one another because the connection we experience makes us care. It's far easier to share, brainstorm, and be creative in an environment in which each wants the other to realize their potential. Although each brings their cherished principles and standards, there's a healthy non-attachment. They are more passionate about getting something right than they are about getting their own way. The wonderful synergy that results leads to more efficient work habits, not to mention innovation. The result is a high quality of work that's driven by a love of what we're doing.

The Centrality of Heart Connection

Awakened relationships evidence awareness of the heart connection between people. Kindness pervades and people genuinely care for one another. This is because, when the mind becomes quiet, a sense of spaciousness emerges and reveals our inherent interconnectedness. Thus when we help another, it feels as if we're helping ourselves. When we share with another, we feel we're sharing with a greater part of ourselves. A natural reciprocity occurs, reflecting the truth of our situation, which is that our own wellbeing and success depend on the wellbeing and success of the other.

When we are present in each moment instead of off in our thoughts or caught up in an emotional reaction, the experience of presence imbues each person and occasion with a sacredness. Unsurprisingly, each perceives the relationship as precious and not to be dishonored.

When a connection is caring, kind, heartfelt, sharing, and sacred, it has all the hallmarks of love. Do you have the courage to embrace the word "love," even in a business relationship? If you feel deeply relaxed, open, and expanded in the chest area, it will be easier to embrace this word as part of your business vocabulary.

Fully embodying our heart requires more than projecting our feelings outward in expressions of caring and kindness. It requires a willingness to be affected, to have our heart touched by the other. An important aspect of this is to not be defensive, since to be defensive involves a loss of connection to the other. We resist what's unfolding by resisting the natural state of our own tender heart and the fact of our interconnectedness.

Most of us believe we are protecting ourselves when we close our heart. As a child, when we had less control of our life, this was often an important survival mechanism. When no other option is available, a child develops strategies to negotiate traumatic situations. The particular strategies chosen often reflect a child's natural personality tendencies. For example, a friendly, communicative child may learn to keep others at a distance by entertaining them with jokes or by playing the role of appeaser in a contentious atmosphere. In contrast, a thoughtful, introspective child might protect themselves by withdrawing into their own imagination and limiting social contact.

When we become defensive, in effect our natural gifts become distorted, although we are likely unaware this has happened. Stuck in survival mode, we make an identity out of these distorted behavior patterns, which causes us to stay on the surface in our relationships. This is when fear and a perception of being threatened abound, which, of course, triggers our reflex to resist being affected by one another.

Unless we develop a strong sense of presence, in the workplace it's easy to become overwhelmed by contact with one another, causing us to retreat into our survival patterns and our surface personality. We may tolerate a few moments of real connection here and there, but soon scurry behind our protective layers and the superficial stories we tell ourselves about the other person and the situation.

It's important to realize that we can learn to catch ourselves in the act of retreating out of fear and refocus our attention through the simple act of becoming aware of our body and our breath, which is, of course, what a few moments of meditation facilitates. By getting into the habit of focusing on how our body feels and on our breathing, we realize that feeling more than we are used to feeling isn't at all the same as being overwhelmed. In so many ways, our breath is our deepest and greatest lover—not just the preserver of life, but our primary portal into a quality life.

As we learn not to react, and our camouflage is replaced by heartfelt connection, we become more sincere and open-hearted, and consequently our ability to conceal our beliefs, attitudes, agendas, and fears diminishes. If some wish to flee from our growing authenticity, either by pulling away from our presence or provoking us with negative words or actions, our challenge is to not judge them or use them as an excuse for a response that fails to manifest presence. Instead, we can come to rest in the ground of our being, which will empower us to be patient and gentle with them. After all, our presence doesn't depend on what's happening around us on the surface of reality, but on who we are discovering ourselves to be as we shed our learned childhood defenses.

The heart is naturally compassionate, prompting us to listen more. We also discover how to express ourselves without squashing or reacting to the other's need to express themselves. If we are always preparing to speak and not deeply listening with our entire body, we limit our capacity for compassion. The balance is found by assessing how present we are, which we do by paying attention to our body and breathing. The stronger our sense of presence, the less we will feel pulled out of balance by the urgings of our ego. As we become more in touch with ourselves from moment to moment, we learn to trust a deeper wisdom that intuitively guides us as to when it's time to express ourselves and when it's time to listen. A deeper knowing then guides our giving and receiving.

How Compassion Transforms a Business Environment

A colleague may be saying something in a meeting, in response to which we begin to feel charged emotionally. Their words feel threatening to us and our own view of things. Rather than beginning to tell ourselves a story about the person or what they are saying, which feeds reactivity, we can instead notice its physiological impact. We might observe to ourselves, "There's a knot in my stomach, and my chest feels tight."

When we pay attention to the kinesthetic effects of emotions instead of the stories they trigger in our head, we are less likely to become caught up in drama. Awareness of the effect things have on our body tends to keep us grounded, and hence present, which means we are able to see the other more clearly and deeply. We may even be able to respond compassionately to their viewpoint, whether we agree with them or not.

Making space for emotions means we allow them to be. We see that they are just energy under pressure. There's no need to suppress them, to blunt their impact on us. On the contrary, being rooted in presence and truly sitting with our experience, whatever it is, we realize we have nothing to fear. As our ability to stay connected to people increases, so does the value of the contribution we can make.

Some companies have a few people who form a group that's committed to greater awareness and connection. From this group, a new way of relating and of doing business can spread throughout the company. Ideally such a group consists of people who wish to do this voluntarily. The optimal scenario is to have awakening executives who lead by example, since their heartfelt presence can have a dramatic rippling effect throughout the company and transform its culture.

The scientific evidence for the value of compassion in places of business has increased rapidly and is convincing.[9] Employees who cultivate compassion not only have better working relationships, but they also have a higher level of physical and mental wellbeing. Compassionate employees are happier; giving of ourselves has been proven to be more psychologically and emotionally satisfying than receiving. Compassion also promotes social connectedness, which boosts the immune system. In fact, a University of Wisconsin-Madison study has shown that compassion can be developed with training, and that as compassion training strengthens our altruistic tendencies, it alters our neural responses to suffering.[10] By producing altruistic behavior, it imparts meaning to our lives, which has been shown to reduce inflammation and makes for a happier society. By reaching out of our comfort zone to connect with and care for others, we become less stressed and navel-gazing, both of which are hallmarks of depression and anxiety-prone people. (Here we are making a distinction between self absorption and a healthy introspective self-awareness.)

Companies that engage in "conscious capitalism"—that is, compassionate enterprise—perform ten times better than traditional companies.[11] Executives who cultivate compassion and encourage this in their employees are therefore making one of the soundest investments a business can make.

Compassion makes executives better managers because it results in empathy, which helps them to understand clients, society's needs, and especially employees and their needs. Indeed, when awakened executives come to know themselves, they develop a deeper relationship with employees, clients, and society, which enables the whole company to move forward.

A Cradle of Creativity

When we come from the heart, we read other people more successfully. Because we are tuned into our heart, we don't become passive-aggressive. Neither do we feign interest, but are really engaged and care about what's happening.

To listen deeply to another engages us in internal listening. We are listening to what we really want to say. We are listening to the intelligent field from which the wisest and most appropriate words arise. This requires us to pause during a conversation. When we pause to listen to ourselves, people respect this. They understand we are trying to say something authentic and relevant. We are tuning into our own wisdom, and this predisposes us to tune into and invite their wisdom. Together, we create a field of deep listening that can produce insight and creativity. Listening to ourselves, to the other, and to the field between us is an integral part of effective work relationships.

We have talked about a number of ways the heart plays a central role in the awakened company, but we might want to know how and where to begin. It's worth asking ourselves the following questions concerning connecting from the heart in our business relationships:

1. Is there mutual reciprocity of caring in the relationship?

2. Is there a genuine desire to be together?

3. Is there an authentic desire to learn, grow, and bring out the best in the other person?

4. Is the relationship bold enough to weather the strongest emotions?

5. Is the relationship open to the expression of real desires?

Many of us go through our working day upset a lot of the time. Sometimes things should be talked out because there really is a need for resolution of an issue that involves more than ourselves, and it's more pertinent to the work we are performing and our business relationship than simply reacting to someone or something. If we are just upset, a walk, a short run, or vigorous shaking of our limbs would often serve us better than talking—and certainly better than openly ranting.

Much of the time we react too frequently and too strongly to the simple daily events that challenge us all. We may be stuck in line or in traffic, or a colleague is doing something that irritates us. This is the time to take two or three deep breaths to break up our conditioning and reset our awareness to the here and now. The result is a calmer body and a quieting of the mind—the latter being especially important, since it's the mind that produced the story of being offended or hurt by a colleague in the first place. The challenge of course is to have enough presence to remember that resetting our attention by paying attention to our body and breath is an option to being swept up in our reactions.

Mindfulness, a term we have encountered many times, means we are focused on being a calm, wise witness to our inner experience, as well as to what's currently unfolding. With practice, the effort of mindfulness becomes an effortless presence that helps us disengage from past habits and future speculation, allowing us to approach all situations with fresh eyes. This is particularly important, given that business must always have an eye on the future. Unless we are present now, we are likely to be resistant to change; and if we do look to the future, our predictions and assessments of the future will tend to be some variation of the past or at best guesswork.

By tuning into the field of wisdom that can be accessed in calmness, we create space to receive the future and shape it from a fresh perspective.

In a very real sense, creativity and innovation are the future calling us forward, the future arriving in the now.

It's valuable for colleagues to use a meditative stillness to calm themselves if they find themselves locking horns. Having said this, the first time you and a colleague try to root yourselves in presence, and the upset and reactivity doesn't completely stop, your ego will of course tell you this shifting of awareness isn't working. But with practice, you'll find it brings great change in how you relate.

Remember also that cultivating presence isn't swallowing our reactions. We fully feel the physical reality of our emotions, but without getting caught up in them. If we allow ourselves to feel the emotional energy, without starting an inner commentary about what it means, and without discharging the energy through impulsive words or actions, the reaction will dissipate. We will then see our colleague with the fresh eyes of compassion.

Boundaries as a Facet of Connection

We have said again and again that the hallmark of an enlightened relationship is that we are separate individuals who recognize there's ultimately no separation. Having said this, any relationship requires parameters for smooth functioning. We think of these in terms of the relatedness A, B, Cs. A is for the attitude we wish to bring to the situation. B is for the healthy boundaries we wish to maintain in the relationship. C is for the connectedness between each of the parties.

For instance, there needs to be a reasonable expectation that each party will treat others the way they themselves wish to be treated. Participants on a project need to know they can count on each other for consistent behavior, so that when someone says they will do something, they will carry through. Candidness is also vital, so that we can trust that if someone says they either like or dislike something, they mean what they say. They don't say "yes" to something when they really mean "no."

Certain values, if disrespected, can be deal breakers in a relationship. For example, if a company believes strongly in equality of opportunity and treatment for the sexes, but one of the parties disregards this, there may be a severe clash. A growing relationship can survive this only if each person is open to seeing the world through different eyes. A healthy relationship allows latitude in terms of other perspectives. We may not always agree with another's values, but at a minimum, we need to consider what they imply.

A healthy relationship also allows for imperfections, so that people are willing to forgive one another. After all, humans make mistakes from time to time. However, if one party is in continual need of forgiveness, this needs to be investigated. For example, if someone in a detail-oriented job consistently misses the details and is continually having to apologize, it needs to be asked whether they are in the right role.

An important key to the success of a company's personnel is to place individuals in the right roles, then develop them in these roles. In this way, we work around people's weaknesses and can bring out their strengths. This may seem obvious, but you would be surprised how often, for a variety of reasons, such a basic insight isn't utilized in companies. Awakened executives keep an eye on matching the natural talents and predilections of employees with tasks that allow them to thrive.

As Florian Heiner explains from the point of view of General Manager of a large hotel, "As the leader of the organization, it's my job to unlock my team's confidence, which in turn unlocks their talent. People have abilities they have no clue they possess. Good leadership means getting to know them, familiarizing yourself with their strengths and their weaknesses, as well as their needs. By taking time to be alongside them, joining in activities with them, you discover how you can best empower them. This is what makes for people who are happy in their work."

Heiner goes on to emphasize, "I'm not looking for short-term employees, but for long-term personnel who can be further developed—individuals who are on a career path within our organization. A vital aspect of developing people long-term is to give them room to be themselves. If you don't give them room to be true to themselves, they won't be happy, and then they won't grow. Their potential remains locked within them. But if you unlock your people's potential, this builds positive energy in the company."

This leader is reluctant to let people go, and for good reason. Indeed, when the Crowne Plaza in Jinan, China, went through a major expansion, including the addition of an upscale shopping mall, and construction required closing the facility for several months, Heiner so valued the staff he had developed that not a single one of the hundreds of employees was laid off. Instead, they were put to work in such tasks as watching that construction materials didn't "walk" from the site.

How is it possible to develop such longevity of employment in a company? "Let's say that someone is failing in their job," Heiner explains, "whether because of lack of knowl-edge, lack of time to adjust, or simply because they are in the wrong job. In such a situation, using the coaching model, we try not to push; rather, we want to draw out the best in the individual. We talk with them in a pleasant, non-threatening environment, such as sitting over coffee. We want them to be completely comfortable so that they can share with us what's really going on in their life. Sometimes we learn it's something we are doing wrong as leaders—perhaps not enough training, inconsistency in how we manage, too great a complexity to the job for a single person, or any number of things. We listen, truly seeking to understand. In fact, we learn more from those who wish to resign than from almost anything else. They alert us to where we need to make changes."

What if you've done all you can to coach an individual in a particular role, yet they still aren't working out? Even then, Heiner isn't ready to give up on a staff member. "We see if we can transfer them to another function within the company," he says. "In this way we don't lose the asset we spotted when we initially hired them, and neither do we lose all that we've invested in them. If your company is large, such as this hotel, there may be a role that's far more suitable for the individual. If the person isn't suited for what they are doing—isn't happy and fulfilled in their work—a hotel is a great environment because it's like many industries rolled up into one. There are so many departments in a hotel. Someone may have the right culture in their heart, which is why we hired them, but they perhaps aren't suited to selling—a fact they only learned by trying it. However, as we talk with them, we learn they would fit perfectly into administration. Or someone in administra-tion turns out to be a person who has the kind of personality that thrives on interfacing directly with the customer. We try to give such individuals another platform—a move we find to be successful most of the time. All we are doing is drawing out what we saw in them when we hired them by giving them a place where they can grow."

There's a challenge here to work with people in the organization in a way that recognizes the need for professional roles, keeping in mind that everyone has something of value to bring to the table. If people don't perform, they are offered all the help necessary. If this doesn't work, they can then look for another organization that may be more suited to their particular gifts. For example, I had a job managing a hundred paid-by-the-hour telephone interviewers. I was terrible at it—and to be blunt, pretty ineffectual. My supervisor had the courage to let me know my heart wasn't into it, and it was obvious. A career counselor helped me to select my current path.

15

THE AWAKENED WAY TO HANDLE AN EMOTIONALLY CHARGED MEETING

Much of what we've discussed so far has particular appli-
cation to meetings. Indeed, it could be said that many
of the issues we've addressed come to a head in meetings. It's
in boards, committees, and teams that we seem to showcase
issues.

One element that surfaces in many meetings is any tendency we may have to one-upmanship. Although we have
already addressed such behavior, considering it in the context
of meetings allows us to take our discussion to a deeper level.

Consider the situation in which someone you work with
remarks in a meeting, "I just loved what you said." What
does their comment feel like? Don't focus on what you think
about it. Focus on the physical sensations it generates in your
body. Does it have a warming effect? Do you feel somehow
lighter, more alive? Is there a tingling in parts of your body, a
sensation of excitement?

During the same meeting, someone else puts forward an
idea that contradicts one of yours. What does this feel like?
Do you sense you've been stabbed, wounded, injured? Does it
feel like you are being abused? Is there a spike in your energy,

or a drop in your energy? Do you find yourself feeling pressured, pushed, forced?

When a colleague comments in a meeting, we may find ourselves feeling emotionally charged by what they are saying. Something about their words threatens our own view of things. Our usual reaction tends to be to tell ourselves a story about this person.

But what if we instead noticed how what the person is saying is impacting us physiologically? "Wow, I'm starting to feel flushed and hot under the collar," we might realize. Or perhaps we experience a heavy feeling in our chest and find ourselves getting antsy. As we become aware of the effect the other is having on us physiologically, we can then take the step of recognizing that what they are saying is touching on some unresolved issue in us.

As mentioned in an earlier chapter, whenever we experience an emotional charge in reaction to someone else, it always points to something in ourselves we haven't dealt with. If it didn't, we might not agree with what's said, but we would feel no emotional charge because we don't take it personally.

Becoming aware of when we are experiencing an emotional charge enables us to separate any reaction we may be having to the other from our feelings about them, which in turn allows us to at least understand their point of view, whether we agree with it or not.

If we become still, we perceive a deep peace beneath all our surface interactions. Anchored in this peace, we feel soothed, reassured, and unafraid of tackling the most challenging issues—including those individuals who really know how to push our buttons. We realize that emotional reactions are just energy. There's no need to suppress them in an attempt to blunt their impact on us. They don't have to overwhelm us, take us over. We can simply allow them to pass through us.

Cultivate Inner Stillness in Meetings

To know how to foster a spirit of cooperating with one another in a meeting is a powerful tool that every executive can and should have. The alternative is the difficult and unproductive relationships that are currently strewn across the countless meetings that occur in the business landscape.

A key that a growing number of leaders are using to develop and maintain a sense of working together throughout meetings is the art of entering into stillness. To start meetings in silence is an invitation for synergy to enter the room. As we saw in an earlier chapter, our ability to *pause* before succumbing to automatic impulses, which are usually poorly thought out and consequently negative, equips us to be better listeners, brainstormers, and decision makers. We find ourselves being more receptive to creative possibilities.

If we develop the habit of paying close attention to ourselves and to the relational field, we are naturally moved to be still when the moment calls for it. In an awakened relationship, colleagues value those moments when no words are necessary. No effort is made to fill the silence with banter. There are no uncomfortable moments, and each person feels deeply at ease.

The absolute emptiness of such stillness often dissolves resistance, heals upsets, and allows for something truly creative to emerge. This is because the stillness within each of us, if we are tuned into it, brims with information. So, as touched on earlier, when we free our mind of clutter, pressure, and emotional reactivity, we make space for a deeper life wisdom to emerge.

It's important to point out that inner stillness isn't the same as verbal silence. We can communicate while our mind is relatively quiet, even silent. On the other hand, we can be quiet in a meeting, yet awash with reactions to and critiques of what's being discussed. Because we've come to the meeting preloaded, we can't enter into the inner stillness that allows us to orient ourselves to hearing the other.

Unless we access our inner stillness, rather than merely becoming silent on the surface, it's easy to become triggered during meetings. Because of the way we grew up, many of us easily feel ignored, sidelined, and even put down or attacked. Since we grew up deprived of perceiving our interconnectedness, we had to learn to defend ourselves. As a consequence, we stay on the surface in the way we relate to one another. Unable to access our naturally compassionate center, we fail to understand people and misinterpret much of what takes place between and around us. In this distorted state, fear and threats abound, which causes us to resist being open to those we work among. If we are in a meeting and see a hard stare or distant darting eyes, tensed body language, or the irregular breathing of a colleague whose mind is busily converting thoughts into powerful emotional energy, it may be possible to suggest the group take a breather—though this has to be done with great sensitivity. If there is more widespread tension in the room, we might want to pause and invite everyone to enter into a few minutes of stillness.

When we come from a state of stillness, we tend to read another person more successfully. We are simultaneously sensitive to them, aware of our reactions to them, and tuned into the field between us. Really engaged, we care about what's happening around us—what's happening in the field.

If we ourselves lack a sense of groundedness, we can become overwhelmed by challenges from individuals in the meeting who have strong presence, which will exacerbate any tendency we may have to retreat into our survival patterns. We may tolerate a few moments of what we perceive as the other's overwhelming presence, but then we'll scurry back behind our protective layers and the superficial stories we tell ourselves about the situation. If we can catch ourselves in the act of retreating, we can instead refocus our attention on our breath, which will enable us to stay with the situation without panicking.

When we do so, we discover that feeling the intensity of the other's presence isn't the same as being overwhelmed. It just feels like a bigger flavor than we are accustomed to, but it isn't necessarily a difficult experience. The idea we won't be able to stand it is purely an interpretation we put on it because of the story we tell ourselves about the other. The more times we go through the process of staying present instead of running for cover, we may find we actually like the intense feeling of sustained connection.

In some cases we will learn that, given their current level of awareness, someone is incapable of deep connection. Regardless, our task is neither to judge them nor use them as an excuse for our own inability to remain present. The challenge is always to be centered and grounded. At such times, it may help for you to feel your feet firmly rooted on the ground.

Listen with Your Entire Being

Especially when we feel threatened in some way, there's a tendency not to really listen to another's viewpoint. Certainly we don't listen with our entire being. Often what we do instead is run our old tapes through our head. Instead of listening deeply, our mind is going over the things we've said, what others have said, and how we will interrupt the other. This is why people often don't feel heard, but feel misunderstood.

If you are in a meeting and you're just biding time until it's your turn to speak—or when you find yourself saying things like, "Yes, but"—no real listening takes place, no tuning into the other person or to the field, and hence no openness. Instead of bringing receptivity to the situation, you're waiting to get your licks in.

If we would pause to examine our urgent need to voice our opinion, we would realize that the things we think about incessantly and that come tumbling out of our mouth at such times have a feel of old things repeated—which of course they are, since they are made up of memories and emotions from our past. Rather than being helpful, they are a way of avoiding the openness that's required to move forward.

What's important is the quality of our listening, our receptiveness to the other person. To really be heard is what everybody always hopes for in a relationship. If, as a result of our defensiveness, we are always preparing what we'll say next instead of listening, we limit our ability to be openminded. In contrast, when we are inwardly still, we discover that the intelligence that works through us does a better job of navigating life's challenges than our historic patterns and defensive self-concepts.

The point is to listen to each other from a place of spacious presence, listening *into* this silent field of intelligence. Thus a healthy interaction will contain pauses, both brief and long, between speaking. There will be a pattern of words and silence, words and silence.

To illustrate the importance of being sure we understand what another is saying, when conducting an interview I asked a candidate what she liked to do in her spare time. She said she liked to play with her crotch rocket. I had no clue what a crotch rocket was and could only imagine. Seeing my expression, she asked if I knew what a crotch rocket is. When I replied that I didn't, she apologetically explained, "It's a motorcycle."

Keep in mind that much of the drama people create is a substitute for a lack of connection, and therefore constitutes a cry for attention from someone who is longing for authentic connection, inclusion, and support. By not buying into the drama by reacting to it emotionally, we can direct our attention to truly connecting from the heart.

It should come as no surprise that the desire to learn new concepts and skills also thrives in such a connected, inclusive, supportive atmosphere. Each of us challenges one another to be our best, giving a project our best effort, precisely because we care about one another. Others will accept nothing less from us, as well as inspiring us to accept nothing less from ourselves. Urging each other forward, each member challenges the other to believe in their abilities and to be disciplined and diligent in putting them into action.

Relationships that feed our sense of wellbeing bring out the best in us. Because they are so satisfying, they foster responsibility and accountability. A desire to maintain the synergy and supportive environment that has been created motivates us to hold ourselves to a high standard of conduct. Then, when we at times inevitably fall short of our high standards, we feel compelled—impelled by our natural desire to act with integrity—to be real and truthful with group members, even when it pinches a bit.

Freedom to relax and openly express oneself opens the way to brainstorm projects effectively. Because we feel safe saying what we're thinking—safe putting our true feelings about something out there—we don't worry about risking embarrassment. Such a supportive atmosphere encourages imagination that's freewheeling, outside-the-box, and may just trigger something brilliant as we or others mull over what's being said.

Awareness in Relationships

Sometimes when we are upset or our mind is clouded with worry, we may be tempted to discharge the energy we have allowed to build up within us. Blasting away at someone is never the productive route, particularly in a meeting. It's far more preferable to calmly talk something through, which is a good reason to hold off taking a matter further until the meeting is over and we have an opportunity to talk privately.

Cultivating awareness doesn't mean swallowing or suppressing our reactions. On the contrary, we fully feel the emotions that are arising without getting caught up in them. You may have already heard that emotion is just energy in motion. So let any negative or unpleasant emotion just pass through you. Say to it, "Come-pass-through." Because you don't run a mental commentary concerning what's happening, the discomfort you are feeling then begins to dissipate.

In the course of a normal workday, let alone in an intense meeting when the pressure is on, I find that just in meeting people in hallways or offices, I can so easily react to an individual's idiosyncrasies—even when we meet in passing and nothing is actually said. I have learned that our little stories of hurt and rejection so readily color our view of a person or a situation. Our ego is going to tend to label, critique, and perhaps lash out.

The challenge is to recognize that a viable option to being swept up in an emotional reaction is to have enough presence to pay attention to our breathing and the way our muscles are tightening at such moments. As we consistently practice centering ourselves, whether with one person or among a boardroom of people, doing so eventually becomes instinctive.

To illustrate from my own life, I'm walking through the halls of our business, noticing the actions of different coworkers as I pass their desks and offices. Some behavior catches my attention for a moment longer than other activities. Lost in thought, I'm not aware that my own mood is coloring the way I see what's around me—not aware of what my mind is selectively attracted to, nor aware of the majority of things I unthinkingly choose to ignore. I feel my thoughts pulling me to react, to comment on what's happening, which runs something like, "Same old office every day, back to the grind. Oh, there's so and so, always dropping papers. And that other guy, does he ever stop chatting with everyone? Ah, there's the corporate climber wearing his 'power suit' and no doubt planning his next move."

At this moment, I become aware that I'm caught up in thought. I realize that my mental commentary has little to do with the reality of the moment. As my focus shifts to the simple fact of walking through the office, I feel my unease begin to lift. My breathing relaxes and my gait reflects a drop in muscle tension. I can now distinguish between an event and the meaning I choose to give the event. Papers fall to the ground, people are talking, someone is formally dressed. I realize that no one did anything to me. I did it all to myself. I walk on.

Arriving at my office, I greet my colleague in the usual friendly manner. When there's barely a response, I'm taken aback. Because I was looking forward to a warm greeting, I feel hurt. The key, of course, is to concern myself with my own current level of awareness instead of focusing on my colleague's seeming lack thereof. So before I can become lost in a story about why my colleague isn't being warm to me, I catch myself and take a deep breath. This relaxes me, allowing me to remove my "stuff" from the situation. Because I don't react to my colleague, the feeling of hurt begins to subside, and I find myself free to attend to whatever needs my attention. As the day unfolds as if nothing had happened, I find myself becoming used to being able to simply flow through difficult moments.

16

ACTIVATING, SUSTAINING, AND REGENERATING

Organizations are either going to lead a revolutionary awakening in the way business is conducted on our planet, establishing something more responsible and caring, or they are going to resist—in which case they will become extinct. Business and government have a real opportunity to create a positive ripple.

In Canada, the survivability rate of firms across all sectors and industries is somewhere between 43-52% after three years, 33-40% after five years, and only 20-25% after nine years.[1] In other words, over a ten-year period, roughly 80% of businesses disappear, while a number of those that survive find themselves struggling.[2]

According to a 2013 Gallup poll, only 30% of employees in America—less than one in three—feel engaged at work. Around the world, across 142 countries, the proportion of employees who feel engaged at work is just 13%.[3]

It's also estimated that 33% of all people in the United States have been a victim of nonphysical aggression in the US workforce.[4] Elsewhere, some 75% of Norwegian engineering employees reported experiencing at least one incident of general harassment during a six-month period.[5]

In a groundbreaking study, University of Pennsylvania professor Alexandra Michel took a chilling look at the dark side of life for a modern financier, finding that six out of ten investment bankers suffered serious stress, with many abusing prescription drugs.[6]

The positive effects of organizational health have long been demonstrated.[7] For instance, data shows that the long-term performance of learning organizations in financial markets over time is superior to their competitors, beating the traditional market indexes on a majority of financial measures.[8] Yet most businesses fail on this score, and the human cost to business is huge. In essence, all awakened organizations are learning and adapting continuously.

The Critical Need for Three Different Forms of Energy

There are three points of energetic focus at the organizational level. These involve energizing, sustaining, and regenerating. Of these three modalities, we currently have an imbalanced excess of the energizer and sustaining energies, which are then unfortunately often used for sustaining unawakened practices.

For a successful enterprise, we need all three of these energies. To be an energizer is about qualities such as self-assertion, drive, direction, energy, external adaptation, motivation, focus, goal-orientation, initiating projects, and "making it happen." Many companies already value these qualities as essential for success. The sustaining energy is about maintaining structures and flow, holding to standards, being organized, care, connectedness, values, accountability, responsibility, and anything that has to do with the ordering and support systems of a company. The regenerating energy is much rarer and consists of such elements as the ability to pause and look at the bigger picture, creating space, allowing time for creative processes, and engaging in introspect as needed. It's about innovation, learning, creativity, context, cohesion, and stability. Individuals tend to excel at one of these approaches more than the other, although we can learn to be more skillful at all three. Similarly, companies may favor one of these in their corporate culture; but if one or more of them is missing in significant ways, it spells.

It's because modern businesses suffer from a paucity of regenerative practices that classic American companies often find themselves increasingly marginalized, while others have already gone the way of the dinosaurs. An awakened state is the only way to maintain a diversity of modalities. Without such an awakened state, imbalances in the modalities reoccur again and again.

Businesses require *energizers*, *sustainers*, and *regenerators*.

Employees, relationships, and companies experience greater wellbeing when each of these modalities are included in the workplace. Again, I want to stress that we currently have too many energizers and sustainers. Many companies sorely lack regenerative practices such as time spent in reflection, consideration, analyzing data, working in creative spaces, and working in nature. It's crucial to have a healthy diversity of energies.

Each energizer, sustainer, and regenerator possesses a head, a heart, and a gut. The amalgamation of intellectual intelligence, emotional intelligence, and instinctual or intuitive intelligence represents true awakening. In other words, awakening is multidimensional. Often companies have a dominant energy, with one or two of the attributes emphasized over the others. The key is for organizations to avoid imbalances and to be conscious of what they require at different times, which entails knowing how much energy needs to be expended where and when. When we are balanced, we are better able to cope with the curveballs life throws us that wreak havoc with our plans. We remain centered in the present situation instead of retreating into fearful thoughts, which enables us to act creatively in accordance with what the changed situation requires.

As businesses, we need to be constantly planning and strategizing to maintain and expand our success—in other words, to engage in scenario planning. However, if we aren't present to what's here right now, our assessments and predictions of the future will always be some variation of the past. By tuning into the dynamic *now*, we create space to receive the future and think about it from a fresh perspective.

An awakened executive is someone who has the right combination of expertise, competence, and overarching vision to serve high values. These values will include the cultivation of relaxed groundedness, natural integrity, authenticity, openness, acceptance, humility, truth seeking, meaning, compassion, kindness, intentional awareness and focus, connection, and unity. An executive with these values is equipped to skillfully navigate the interface between the world as it is, the world as it's becoming, and the world that could emerge. These enlightened leaders are able to identify what's real because they aren't affected as much as others by ego and its agenda.

You might wonder whether all of the awakened attributes manifest simultaneously, especially in a public company. In some cases, yes; and in other cases, no. When we trust our awareness to take the helm, the attributes most needed at any given moment naturally come to the fore and express themselves through us. Innovative energy arises when it's most needed, while motivating and harmonizing energy spring to life when required. Energy responds to the true need. This doesn't replace the necessity of learning and skill acquisition, but it guides us toward the skills and information that will be most relevant and useful to our mission.

We may be strong in one attribute, but in order to allow another attribute to grow and express itself through us, we need to "get out of the way" by quieting our mental chatter and emotional reactivity. The intelligence—the conscious-ness—at the core of our being knows what's needed at any given time. It's similar to the way life knows a seed requires different elements and conditions to grow than does a leaf on a mature tree. The intelligence within our body knows what vitamins, minerals, phytonutrients, and so forth are needed by which parts of our system and in what proportion. This intelligence has impeccable timing, building bone, tissue, and skin in abundance as we grow, switching on hormones for reproduction when we enter our teens, setting in motion the birth process when a baby in the womb is fully developed.

This same intelligence is at work in the whole of life if we are attuned to it. Awakened companies and their executives know how to draw on this innate capacity, which, as we've stated several times already, enables them to tap into an open-hearted wisdom that informs their thoughts with regard to the best course of action in any situation.

To illustrate, two business people, one male and the other female, are having lunch together. People often incorrectly assume that if a man and a woman are lunching out and they aren't spouses, something clandestine may be happening. It's the way our minds tend to automatically jump to programmed conclusions. It takes a while to see just how many of these unconscious assumptions we make, and often act on.

Awakened People Take the Initiative

Awakened companies feel no need to "follow the pack." Neither do they shy away from big ideas. They can respect traditional thinking, but they aren't bound by it. In contrast to the many companies that operate according to suffocating rules and protocols, they do things their own way and encourage initiative in their personnel. It's important not to be too rule-bound, constantly pointing out infractions, morally narrow, or inflexible and restrictive.

When there are too many rules, or rules are too strictly enforced, doubt and worry can consume a lot of people's energy, especially those who have a greater need to feel secure. There can also be a lot of changes in policies and project decisions when a company is rule-bound, leading to people not really knowing where they stand or things in general stand.

The difference between being part of an innovative company and a moribund company is huge. In my own case, I was part of one of the largest search firms in the world. Seeing how business was conducted, I yearned to do things a new way. Because this wasn't encouraged, I finally left. The people I worked with were amazing; it was the context that left me feeling constrained. Today, I encourage people in our firm to own who they are, and I endeavor to support their initiative.

Companies with a lot of initiative engage in strategic risk-taking. Their employees don't sit around waiting for someone's edicts. Instead, they manifest an abundance of self-starter energy and full-on engagement. Teams are direct and real with one another. However, it's important to bear in mind that directness isn't the same as bluntness and always has an element of sensitivity to it.

When there is insufficient innovative energy, individuals don't like to upset the apple cart by sharing their perceptions. For this reason, the focus must be on developing a way for participants to speak their mind and feel that what they have to contribute matters. Management mustn't feel threatened if someone needs to take a stand on an issue. If something isn't working, those who perceive this need to feel free to speak up and say it isn't working.

Working from this insight, as awakened companies grow, their employees grow right along with them as individuals are given more responsibility and increased independence. Team managers and leaders help their employees step out of their comfort zone, encouraging them to add their vision and action plans for new projects.

How to Avoid Burnout

It's important to understand that a company can burn itself out if it draws only on energizer energy. There can also be a tendency for some to become bullies, ignoring calls for deliberation and reflection on the part of those who see the need for the company to acknowledge its dependence on those it serves, including all stakeholder groups. Surrendering to the truth of our collective interdependence shows a wisdom with regard to life's processes. We recognize there are forces greater than the company's sheer will. Holding the paradox involves knowing when to act and when to sit back, listen, and consider.

A balance of all three energies—energizing, sustaining, and regenerating—is crucial. When there's too much energizing going on, cooperation begins to suffer. Pretty soon the company starts to look like a bunch of fiefdoms, with everyone pushing their own agenda. None of this supports a sense of cohesion and cooperation within the team. In this reduced awareness of the collective human field, which naturally induces reciprocity, power plays abound and there is less honoring of other people's contributions.

When leaders or employees are constantly pushing forward and disregarding the collective, they can develop tunnel vision that creates a narrow view of what a project needs. When this occurs, it's to the detriment of the overall trajectory and vision of the company and may even expose it to unnecessary risk. The line between bold initiative and recklessness can be a fine one. With an excess of goal-oriented energy, such companies tend to become opportunistic, often trying to ruin competitors. Ironically, in their quest to take others down, they frequently end up ruining themselves.

When imbalances proliferate, the passive become more passive and withdrawn, while the aggressive push ahead and listen even less to anyone else, and the company eventually finds itself running on empty. With personnel who are detached and emotionally numb, there may be rampant dishonesty in the service of profit as the only purpose.

Having warned of the dangers of too much energizing, it's equally important to be aware that it doesn't work to tell a team you want them to take the initiative, then slap them down when they do. People don't like to be micromanaged and may become scared and shut down as a result. Part of creating a humane workplace is to trust colleagues, empowering them by encouraging freedom, flexibility, and a sense of community. In the spirit of inquiry, teams need their latitude and need their autonomy to be respected to explore and investigate things. As Jamie Naughton of Zappos explains, the company gives its employees the freedom to try and fail. They are invited to bring their ideas in-house and make things happen. On the other hand, neither does it work if a team doubts you will actually let them take the initiative because you allow a few to dominate meetings and projects.

When a company begins to feel preoccupied with rules, or becomes rigid, overly logical, too orderly, too detail oriented, or overly conscientious, it has become wedded to the *concept* of integrity and no longer *embodies* it. In fact, it lacks integrity, since integrity requires all aspects to be considered and integrated.

For this reason, the energy of taking the initiative is a powerful one that must be harnessed and directed carefully, then balanced with the energy of sustaining and reinvigorating. These energies must work together synergistically if a company is to enjoy health, prosperity, and longevity.

As Patrick Lencioni points out, "Once organizational health is properly understood and placed in the right context it will surpass all other disciplines in business as the greatest opportunity for improvement and competitive advantage. Really."[9]

Sustainers

Sustainers shape the capacity of the internal alignment of the organization. Awakened companies bring out the best in sustainers so that they are more than just efficient functionaries. They thrive by sharing objectives that are supported by the company culture and climate. Because they enjoy meaningful connection and have worthy values, they are altruists who are focused on service, implementation, and maintaining and adjusting work protocols to keep the organization in alignment.

In other words, sustainers are the *spine* of the organization. Unfortunately, the kind of sustainers who currently dominate businesses tend to be the organizational types. The consequence of having too many energizers, augmented with sustainers whose emphasis is organization, is that unawakened practices get energized, then sustained. Too much of maintaining structures and flow, holding standards, and being organized works against the third crucial aspect of a company that thrives, which is regeneration. However, with a little support from awakening executives, the higher aspects of sustaining can come through, balancing the situation.

To see how this works, consider a company that makes rubber gloves. If the company is awakened, it's not just about providing the rubber gloves. It's about protecting the health of both the patient and the doctor, along with preventing infectious diseases from spreading in our communities. The company is committed to providing a service that really helps others, and consequently the personnel are proud of their efforts.

Awakened companies are concerned with far more than just their products. For instance, can we be considered an effective company if we aren't paying a living wage, providing health and other benefits, pursuing high environmental standards, and expecting the same from our suppliers? All these are part of what it takes to sustain an effective workforce.

Always trying to get by with how little we can pay, limiting ourselves to the "going rate," instead of asking how much we can afford to pay, fails the awakened company test—as does choosing the cheapest option for suppliers, or outsourcing work largely because of the low wages outsourcing generally requires, the chance to avoid paying benefits, and lax environmental standards.

A brazen lack of care for others and the environment reflects a lack of self-awareness on the part of company leadership. However, other than money in our pocket (at least in the short-term), the gains from remaining unawakened are sparse. Our disconnection from our deeper nature leaves us short on personal fulfillment, while the unawakened companies we lead ultimately become less profitable, prone to bankruptcy, and increase the risk of the community in which they operate collapsing economically—and possibly society itself, as we saw with the financial scandal of 2008. Indeed, this is precisely why a small number have grown increasingly wealthy over the past few decades, while the middle class who once enjoyed a pleasurable lifestyle are increasingly being squeezed and in danger of disappearing.

If employee physical and mental health suffers, corporate health suffers. Ailing individuals and a weakened company are in no position to give their best to clients and suppliers, let alone to society. People who feel socially isolated suffer a myriad of physical consequences.[10] Thus when a company is providing the highest care and service for its employees, creating authentic community, it's by extension being caring to those outside of it.

If you consider the service industry, such as hotels, restaurants, dry cleaners, retail, and the like, there's both a relational quality and an anticipatory quality to the energy of caring. We certainly notice when there's an absence of care, as in the case of a distracted waiter who spills soup or red wine on us. To provide quality care and service, a person needs to be alert, with their mind unoccupied by other concerns and fully present in what they are doing.

If we are an awakened service person, customers can sense the extra attention they are receiving from us, since we aren't lost in thought but are focused on what we are doing. Because we aren't distracted by mental chatter or emotional reactivity, the person we're helping doesn't feel like an afterthought and may be amazed by how their needs are anticipated. This builds a sustainable business as customers are drawn back again and again.

Quality care and service originate from within. Cultivating compassion and self-awareness is the way to care for ourselves, serve a higher purpose, and by extension care for and serve our colleagues and the wider community. As awakened individuals, we care for and support each other even when no one is looking and no clients or suppliers are present. We do so for no other reason than the fact we are members of the human race.

Sustainers foster organizational connectedness to the community and to the broader ecosphere. They bring a personable atmosphere to the enterprise. This is the mental aspect of sustainers, the ability to create structures and processes that build community. This attribute is evident in the way we experience each other's generosity, grace, appreciation, maintenance of appropriate boundaries, sharing, checking in with each other, and being attuned to non-verbal cues such as the eyes, facial expressions, body language, and voice intonation.

Regenerators

A CEO confided, "I sat in the parking lot with my face in my hands, so burnt out I wasn't sure I could continue. I considered ending it all right then. I had all the material wealth I could ever need, as well as a supportive family, yet I felt completely unfulfilled. Not only was I unhappy, but my work, which was for the sake of simply making money, wasn't meaningful. What everyone calls the 'intangible benefits' turned out to be the most real of all."

What this CEO needed was the ability to *regenerate*.

The Dalai Lama got it right when he declared, "The planet does not need more successful people. The planet desperately needs more peacemakers, healers, restorers, storytellers, and lovers of all kinds." These are qualities exuded by effective regenerators.

Regeneration is a challenge for those used to leading and activating companies, as can be seen in the case of another CEO who had recently given most of the management of the business to his company's leadership. As he grew increasingly restless, not knowing what to do with his time, it became a source of anger and frustration for him. Regeneration simply wasn't part of his repertoire.

Regeneration involves an ongoing ability to experiment and try different ideas and modalities that simplify and improve existing practices. Awakened companies have an adaptability and flexibility that allows them to pivot rapidly from big picture strategizing to scrutinizing minute details. To fulfill this role, regenerators need to be aware of subconscious trends, both individual and collective. This enables outside-the-box thinking, which is a vital part of a regenerator's culture—although, unlike the work of energizers, it takes place within the context of discipline and competence.

Regeneration is closely linked to innovation. As part of regeneration, the creative brainstorming process by individuals and teams needs to be ongoing throughout the process of innovation, shaping and refining ideas at each successive stage.

However, unlike the energizing aspect of a company, which can foster creativity simply for creativity's sake, the energy of regeneration is more concerned with the implementation of the best ideas that emerge and are applicable to the current situation. Following the implementation of a prototype policy or product, regenerators will also see to it that these are fine-tuned until the company is satisfied it has met its own high standards.

Beginning with Nothing

How can a company pursue a program of regeneration?

Well, let me ask you, which do you lean more toward—having a strict agenda, or having no agenda at all? Since there's a balance to be had between form and free-flowing in organizations, how can you bring more of the opposite of your personal preference to your teams?

In our company, we began one team transformation with a statement that we had no agenda for this meeting, followed by a five-minute meditation. Then we let the team set the agenda in the moment. It was an uncomfortable experience for someone used to agendas. To have an agenda or refrain from setting one should be dependent on what's most needed at the particular time for the team's maximum performance.

To kickstart the regeneration of your company, you might experiment by trying a meeting with no agenda, followed by one with a strict agenda. For example, Google's Genius Hour isn't motivated solely by profit but is used for research for investigation's sake.[11] Following this, you can then think about which worked best for you, and why. Is there room for you to have both types of meetings, and can you see how both would be beneficial? What type of meeting would your team members prefer, and what might their reasons be?

Clothing designers tend to have a lot of regenerative energy, which fosters respect for both individual style and diversity. There's a mix of individual contributions and the collective efforts of a creative team, with an emphasis on valuing both. Some tech companies also have this vibration—for example, Apple, with their sleekly designed products. Having unique and well-thought-out product designs and work environments affects the bottom line.[12]

Dr. Julian Barling concludes, "After five or six decades, I think we just have to realize once and for all that extrinsic factors such as pay and benefits are ultimately poor motivators. They don't get us where we need to go. In fact, they never did. When we pay people really well, what we often find is that the people who we wish would leave, stay; whereas the people who are really contributing get paid more to go elsewhere. In other words, pay often helps organizations maintain the status quo. What we want aren't people who do what they do because they have to. What we want are people who do what they do because they want to. We want people who do what they have to do for sure, but love doing it. I'm deliberately trying to emphasize the word 'love.' They love what they do."

We were working with a tax team from one of the top five accounting firms internationally, and the person who had the most tax breakthroughs was the one who studied issues in depth, allowing the team to leverage his insight into the various tax acts. In a similar manner, for teams to leverage non-linear problem-solving involves considering and "feeling into" issues that are outside the box, in essence coloring outside the lines with the kind of contribution that springs from a strong intuition or a flash of inspiration.

We saw in an earlier chapter how all great ideas, whether we are aware of this or not, come from beyond the thinking mind. Even dreams, visions, and eureka moments come from the silent space that gives birth to all forms, including thoughts. To access them requires as it were "feeling the back of the body." It's as if we are physically and psychologically leaning back, purposefully becoming receptive to the creative flow that comes from the silent, still place within.

Regeneration has an aesthetic element, involving design, beauty, and consideration given to both individual and collective lifestyles. Efforts to reduce or eliminate toxic paint, along with cheap fluorescent lighting that can be toxic to our creative soul, help create a humane and humanizing environment that feels warm and beautiful.

As part of regeneration, aesthetic energy helps us sink into a deeper place, where time both to think alone and to brainstorm is valued. Conversations will be deep in organizations that have a lot of this energy. If the aesthetic element isn't present in abundance in an organization, the company will fail to promote an emotionally cathartic culture, a safe space to explore beyond the edges of "normal." The organization will then feel stale, clinical, and not very creative.

When regenerative energy is in short supply, individuals won't be honored, whereas overly collective group-think will rule. There will also be a sense of meaninglessness. In your organization, is individuality and uniqueness celebrated and welcomed?

Valuing individuality is the trait I see least in organizations. It needs to be encouraged. Some practical aids to supporting it include activities such as having everyone develop their own creativity cards that define them. You could have cards with one word written on them or a picture that represents the individual. Then, allow individuals to contribute in their unique ways to create team graffiti.

There are many fun and effective ways to explore this. As discussed in an earlier chapter, encourage individual artwork in offices. Allow music in the workplace. In fact, go a step further and hire a violinist or harpist one day. Then have different scent days (provided no one has allergies to scents!). Having a unique day of such rituals during which people share some of their experiences increases the group bond through the sharing of each person's uniqueness. You can also have an outdoors day, yoga pose days, each one teach one days, and dress up or down days on which people are encouraged to share their uniqueness.

To foster the energy of regeneration, insert pauses in your calendar, as Kaae in Denmark does. And as Solomon at Renewal Funds encourages, actively brainstorm ways to reduce the war analogies associated with your organization, with their relentless focus on "beating the competition," when the competition could so much better be your neighbor or friend.

Especially, cultivate an atmosphere of inner stillness in your workplace, whereby it becomes a sanctuary. To encourage this, let there be brief periods when silence is everywhere. If possible, create a meditation room. And in the normal course of your interactions, don't go filling in the empty space, recognizing instead that it's there for a reason. Breathe together. Be wordless together.

Change the environment of your company in these and similar ways, and you'll be surprised by the results. People are intuitively and biologically aware of unbalanced, unjust environments.

It's now time for business to come from a place of *being*, where energizing, sustaining, and regeneration are all encouraged. It's a linear and nonlinear, circular practice, and it's about the quality of our experiences along the way. In a nutshell, we are talking about becoming so deeply in touch with the present moment that the circumstances are simply there for our learning. Are we open enough to realize this and allow ourselves to experience it? If we are, it will change our perception of what really matters. We will experience economic good times and down times, but the more fundamental question is, were we present for them?

TOWARD AN AWAKENED ECONOMY

Pamela Jeffery, Founder of WXN, the Women's Executive Network, remarked, "We do have a militaristic hierarchical approach to how we run businesses and government, it's unfortunate." Historically, economies were largely defined by a feudal system. In feudal times, legal and military power enforced a social structure centered around relationships derived from the holding of land in exchange for service or labor.

Today, two quite different economic systems are dominant—a more capitalistic system and a more socialist system. Capitalism is an economic and political system in which a country's trade and industry are controlled by private owners for profit, rather than by the state. Capitalism without a stronger government hand has been shown to benefit the few. Socialism, on the other hand, advocates that the means of production, distribution, and exchange should be regulated by the community as a whole. This is about common ownership. I suggest that a new system—not a blending of the two systems, but a brand new vision and approach—is necessary to create a society that's awake enough to address the global problems we are facing. Such a system will allow us to accomplish things that these earlier systems have been unable to accomplish.

As Pamela Jeffery remarks, "Elevated more awake companies will embrace the opportunity to understand different kinds of governance models in a world where corporate social responsibility is much more at the forefront and companies are expected to engage in stakeholder consultations not only for the good of the company but for the benefit of society."

Presently, our economies are tied to growth, with Gross Domestic Product as our main barometer of how we are doing. As things stand, society may have a few brief periods of compassionate reciprocity during which many people benefit, but such boom times never last long because the tendency of the human ego is to move toward fear, expediency, and greed over the long run. Consequently, no sooner do people begin to enjoy a little prosperity and satisfaction in their work than the downward spiral of selfish hoarding, controlling, and expedient behavior predictably increases—until the little boom becomes a bust once again.

Throughout *The Awakened Company*, we have seen that economic growth is only one measure of wellbeing. Since it often comes at the cost of endangering our own survival, there are other, more preferable standards we should take into account.

Highlighting how these more preferable standards would benefit us all, Jeff Rubin in *The End of Growth* concludes, "The surprising thing is that if we look at it through a different lens, the end of the growth will leave us all richer than we ever may have thought."[1]

The ego, which is the driving force of much of the modern economy's emphasis on growth, tends to be endlessly dissatisfied and always wanting more. Because it perceives others as separate, it's inclined to view them as an obstacle, if not a threat, to what it wants. For this reason, the reign of the ego in the world of business needs to be superseded by the compassion and wisdom that flow from an awareness of our interdependence and interconnection. Such awareness is the *only* real antidote to an economy plagued with boom-bust cycles. Seeking to complete itself, the ego looks to the "next thing" in the material world to accomplish this. However, its effort is utterly futile, since this "next thing" leads only to continuing failure to experience fulfillment, requiring yet the "next." The ego can't grasp that it is the impediment to fulfillment.

When the cry is for constant growth, the business community becomes a battlefield littered with employees and CEOs who are lost. What they don't realize is that, lost though they may be, they are actually a mere breath away from self-fulfillment. All that's required is a courageous look inward that can reveal a higher purpose, augmented with a heartfelt reaching out to others, whereby we regard them as colleagues instead of as competitors. These two simple shifts are all that's required to start us down the path toward a restored economic trinity of family, community, and business.

What a difference it would make if this trinity were in place in economies throughout the world. To take just one example of how humanity would benefit, consider how the current business model has produced more than a few companies whose management would never live downwind or downstream from the pollution their company creates—the by-product of neglect, lack of concern, and detachment from their own community. They would rather spend huge dollars on convincing the community that it always needs one more product or service, instead of seeing what's needed for the physical, mental, and spiritual health of people.

There's absolutely no reason any business can't function from a baseline of noble intent, producing something with meaning in a manner that's humane. This isn't a new idea.

"Business as Usual" Is a Betrayal of Our Humanity

The awakened company is a reflection of the growing awareness of the value of each member of the human race. Science has shown us we are all part of a single fabric of space-time, which means it's no longer just a nice "spiritual" notion to state that we are interconnected, interdependent, and ultimately one. It's a hard fact that needs to strongly influence every decision we take, every move we make.

We have all seen abundant evidence of why it's detrimental not only to individual businesses, but also to the entire world, for a company to give into the most base of impulses, as happened with organizations such as Lehman Brothers and Enron. We can no longer subscribe to the lie that a working life focused on profit at any cost will fulfill us.

In the current prevalent business world, because the majority of us are disconnected from our true self and therefore from one another, we feel incomplete and are always seeking more of everything. This lack of satisfaction leads to greed, oppression, depression, and even violence as we attempt to right our imbalance.

When we are aware, we are able to go beyond randomly hoping for and envying the attributes of others. We can also go beyond the basic set of attributes we were born and raised with. The key to helping us reset ourselves and open up to new attributes is to be aligned with our common oneness. The awakened executive and employee realize we aren't the voices in our head, the volatile emotions in our heart, or the physical tensions in our body—all elements that are only aspects of our humanity. When we are awakened, we clear away the clouds of mental chatter and emotional agitation that prevent our ultimate oneness shining through and our connection emerging. We realize we are each an individual expression of the creative energy that animates us all.

It's this sense of ourselves, rather than the ego, that I have in mind when I speak of our "true self." Sadly, too few of us on the planet are at all aware that we have a true self that's different from being in ego. Referring back to her first experience as a prime time host on national Danish television, appearing before 20 million viewers, Kirsten Stendevad relates how people kept telling her, "You just have to be yourself." The fact that people were saying this to her got her thinking. "What does it mean?" she asked herself. "Why do people have to say that to you?" As she pondered this, it became clear that she was being herself when she was "congruent with and in alignment with her soul."

A Business Is a Vehicle for Individual Expression

The awakened company is *a structure designed to reflect how the awakened individual feels,* and the field that it generates includes the relatedness of the company's members and their relationships therein.

Awakening as a company makes all the difference. Writing in the Harvard Business Review, Matthew and Terces Engelhart, creators of Café Gratitude, comment, "When we started our first restaurant in 2004, our goal was to create a place where people wanted to not just eat but also to work. Just like Southwest Airlines or Starbucks, we recognized that a happy staff means happy customers and a more productive, profitable business. But what would this employee-centric vision look like in practice? We decided to start at the beginning—the moment our servers, cooks, baristas and bakers walk through the front door—with a 'clearing' exercise inspired by Eastern meditation and yoga practice. People partner up and ask each other two questions. One is designed to pin point any distracting thoughts or emotions (for example, 'What's bothering you today?'), the other to bring people into the positive 'present' (for example,'What are you grateful for?')."[2]

This approach shows an appropriate valuing of each person in the company. It in effect invites everyone to play their part to the max in whatever role they fill. Thus, in an awakened company, everyone has a deep sense of their contribution to the firm. Every contribution is unique, and hence neither greater than, lesser than, nor equal to another's. Indeed, no one's effort is ever identical to another's. We all contribute from our once-in-a-universe perspective.

Having said this, I suggest that in an awakened company there is less of a discrepancy in pay scale between the most senior people in the firm and the most junior. There's a sense of equality and fairness in how people are rewarded monetarily, based on objective metrics such as actual impact on the organization, potential impact on the organization, education, experience, and attitudes brought to the organization. There still is a difference in compensation, but it just isn't as wide, and no one is paid less than a decent living. This isn't such an outrageous idea and is already in place in some of the most vibrant economies in the world.

In the circular structure of an awakened company, people can lead from behind, lead from the sides, and lead from the middle. This allows everyone to bring about shifts in the company. Since every individual's inherent creative energy longs to express itself, this is the natural way of things. For a hierarchy to squelch this energy or dam it up is contrary to nature and actually requires considerable energy.

As Jeffrey Pfeffer and Robert Sutton explain, "It takes lots of effort and emotional energy to leave one's essential nature at the workplace door—be it a physical or electronic door. And it is simply impossible for many of the best people to stifle their true selves. Instead of trying to get people to be different from what and who they are, skilled leaders let people know what the organizational objectives are, paths for achieving those objectives, and then to the extent possible, help people find, design, and perform roles that move the organization toward those objectives."[3]

Since a corporation would be nothing without employees, and the energy and value of a corporation is equal to the quality of the energy and value of the employees, where do shareholders and owners fit into this picture?

The strongest shareholders and owners are those who, recognizing how much the success of a company depends on the quality of its employees, are willing to support the development of employees. As Pfeffer and Sutton argue, "It's not by accident or coincidence that many of the most successful consistently best-performing companies have CEOs who aren't outrageously overpaid—Amazon.com, Costco, and Southwest Airlines are just a few current examples. By sending a signal that performance is a collective, not just an individual, endeavor, those companies are more likely to induce thought, creativity, and effort on the part of their people."[4]

Beyond Gross Domestic Product

In the existing economic system, we've all heard of executive stress, with its accompanying heart attacks and so forth. But it's not generally realized that, while many women today excel as leaders, the system as it's presently conceived tends to be even harder on them than on males.

Dr. Julian Barling comments, "We now know, for example, that when women do attain executive positions, they tend to experience more stress, enjoy less autonomy and job satisfaction, and receive fewer rewards for the same level of production than do their male counterparts, thus limiting the subsequent likelihood of success and promotional possibilities. Relatedly, women are significantly more likely to leave management positions than men, and when they do choose to leave the organization they have the same reasons that male leaders do, just more of them."[5]

Our current economic system has become like a tree rotting from infestation with ants. The holes in the tree represent what's eaten out of the system by greed, hostile competition, and control of the many by a few. Day by day, lurching from crisis to crisis, boom to bust, the ants keep on munching away.

Some service providers, like investment bankers and even executive search firms, have been eating out a big chunk of the tree via the large percentage of compensation they have been taking for making deals. While I believe such elements add value, the question for me is how much *real* value they have added. Are they truly contributing to the awakening of society?

It's my hope that, eventually, shareholder activism will reduce the amount of compensation both investment bankers and executives take home, and then something hopefully more awakened will emerge. This will cause a fundamental reset of the existing corporate system.

Finally, it needs to be said that, thankfully, not everyone sees the world the same way many of us in the industrialized world see it. Indeed, they think our way of managing an economy is strange. To me, that there are those of our fellow humans who hold a very different view of things is cause for hope. Let me conclude by telling you about one such group of people.

Sheltered in the Himalayas for centuries, it's said that when Bhutan decided to find out what lay beyond its borders, it sent young people to schools around the world. They returned and told the king what they had learned. To Bhutan, a standard such as GDP seemed illogical. Instead, the country chose to measure itself by a different yardstick: Gross National Happiness.

Juxtaposed against growth-chasing economies and rising global temperatures, it's a comforting story—indeed, a beacon for the future, when the world's businesses are at last awakened. However, we need to go beyond thinking in terms of happiness, since happiness is fleeting. Life includes times that are truly challenging and not necessarily happy. It's a *quality* experience that we are really craving, involving the depth of our learning and the value of our contribution as part of a meaningful real economy. Fulfillment lies in performing work that fulfills a deeper function for not only ourselves but also others.

Whether you are a leader in business or part of a team, how meaningful is your life? In terms of your work and its material rewards, do you find that you have much going on, perhaps with considerable success, yet feel dissatisfied? If so, we need you to wake up and transform your company. In this way, you will fulfill yourself and fulfill your potential. The world needs awakened executives, their relationships, and their companies to heal us, advance us as a species, and at the same time save the planet.

Are you ready to bring your head, your heart, and your gut into the equation of energizing, sustaining, and regenerating?

ENDNOTES

Chapter 1

1. U.S. Department of Treasury, *The Financial Crisis Response. In Charts,* April 2012. Retrieved from http://www.treasury.gov/resource-center/data-chart-center/Documents/20120413_FinancialCrisisResponse.pdf.

2. Melissa McInerney, Jennifer M. Mellor, and Laren Hersch, "Recession Depression: Mental Health Effects of the 2008 Stock Market Crash," Stanford, n.d. Retrieved from http://www.stanford.edu/group/scspi/_media/working_papers/McInerney-etal_Recession-Depression.pdf.

3. Dr. Harish Hande founded Selco Solar. Selco won the Ashden Award for Sustainable Energy in 2005 and the Accenture Economic Development Award the same year. In 2007, Selco won the Ashden Award again, presented by former Vice President of the United States Al Gore. On this occasion the award was for outstanding achievement in the energy sector. Hande was named the social entrepreneur of the year 2007 by the Schwab Foundation for Social Entrepreneurship and the Nand & Jeet Khemka Foundation. In 2008, Hande was chosen by Business Today as one of the 21 young leaders for India's 21st century. Later, in June 2008, India Today named him one of the 50 pioneers of change in India.

4. Hande Harish, "Harish Hande: India Can Show The Right Way To Do Business," Feature/Third Anniversary Special, *Forbes India,* May 19, 2012. Retrieved from http://forbesindia.com/article/third-anniversary-special/harish-hande-india-can-show-the-right-way-to-do-business/32936/1.

5. Mac Van Wielingen was a founder of ARC Financial in 1989 and ARC Resources Ltd. in 1996. ARC Financial is a leading private equity investment management company focused on the oil and gas sector in Canada with currently approximately $4 billion of capital under management. Van Wielingen is chairman of the board of directors of ARC Resources Ltd., a past and current director of numerous other companies within the oil and gas sector, and is active in various capacities in the community and the not-for-profit sector. Van Wielingen is a member of the board of directors of Alberta Investment Management Corporation, a provincial crown corporation responsible for managing approximately $70 billion on behalf of public sector pension, endowment and special purpose funds. Mac is also president of Viewpoint Capital Corporation, a private family-owned investment company, and president of Viewpoint Foundation, a private charitable

foundation. In 2011, Van Wielingen won the Prairies Ernst and Young Entrepreneur of the Year award. Van Wielingen is also a founder and chair of the Canadian Centre for Advanced Leadership in Business (CCAL), at the Haskayne School of Business. CCAL's mission is to support the introduction of advanced understandings of business leadership into business education, with a focus on both performance and ethics.

6. Dr. C. Otto Scharmer is a senior lecturer at MIT and founding chair of the Presencing Institute. Scharmer chairs the MIT IDEAS program and helps groups of diverse stakeholders from business, government, and civil society to innovate at the level of the whole system. He co-founded the Global Wellbeing and Gross National Happiness (GNH) Lab, which links innovators from Bhutan, Brazil, Europe, and the United States in order to innovate beyond GDP. He is working with governments in Africa, Asia, and Europe and has delivered award-winning leadership and innovation programs for clients including Alibaba, Daimler, Eileen Fisher, Fujitsu, Google, Natura, and PriceWaterhouse. Scharmer introduced the concept of "presencing"—learning from the emerging future—in his bestselling books *Theory U* and *Presence* (the latter co-authored with P. Senge, J. Jaworski, and B. S. Flowers). His new book *Leading From the Emerging Future: From Ego-system to Eco-system Economies* (co-authored with Katrin Kaufer) focuses on transforming business, society, and self (published in July 2013). He currently is a vice chair of the World Economic Forum's Global Agenda Council on New Leadership Models and holds a Ph.D. in economics and management from Witten-Herdecke University in Germany. The founder of Theory U and the subsequent website—www.presencing.com—Scharmer has extensive experience working with some of the world's leaders in business, government, and civil society using Theory U and the presencing process to teach groups and organizations how to develop holistic leadership capabilities and capacities.

7. Craig Kielburger has shared the stage, and his voice, with Nobel Peace laureates, heads of state, celebrities, rock bands, actors and pop icons, including former president Clinton, former Soviet leader Mikhail Gorbachev, Archbishop Desmond Tutu, Sir Richard Branson, and many more. With his brother, Marc, Craig writes "Global Voices," a weekly column about the pressing issues of our time, syndicated in the Vancouver Sun, Halifax Chronicle Herald, Calgary Herald, Edmonton Journal, Winnipeg Free Press, The Huffington Post and Huffington Post Canada online. The Kielburgers also write a weekly advice column in the Globe & Mail called, "Ask the Kielburgers." Craig is a New York Times bestselling author who has written nine books. His latest is *Living Me to We: The Guide for Socially Conscious Canadians*. He has a degree in peace and conflict studies from the University of Toronto and is the youngest-ever graduate of the Kellogg-Schulich Executive MBA program. He has received 15 honorary doctorates and degrees, The Roosevelt Freedom From Fear Medal, The World's Children's Prize for the

Rights of the Child, and is one of the youngest recipients of The Order of Canada. Craig's work has been featured on multiple appearances on The Oprah Winfrey Show, CNN, 60 Minutes, Piers Morgan Live, and The Today Show; and in People, Time, and The Economist.

8. Henry Mintzberg is a world renowned academic and author specializing in business and management. Henry Mintzberg, *Wikipedia, The Free Encyclopedia,* n.d. Retrieved from http://en.wikipedia.org/wiki/Henry_Mintzberg. Author of 16 books and nearly 160 articles, Mintzberg is currently the Cleghorn Professor of Management Studies at McGill University. Henry Mintzberg, *Résumé,* n.d. Retrieved from http://www.mintzberg.org/resume. He published *Managers not MBAs* in 2004, *Tracking Strategies* in 2007, and *Simply Managing* in 2013. Mintzberg shares our sense of urgency in rebuilding companies as communities. He is also known for his controversial views on management education and training; views that are becoming far less contentious as people wake up to the failures of our current business model.

9. George Ivanovitch Gurdjieff was an early 20th century author and teacher whose work revolved around the concept that most humans live in a state of hypnotic "waking sleep."

10. Jeffrey Pfeffer and Robert Sutton, *Hard Facts, Dangerous Half Truths & Total Nonsense, Profiting from Evidence Based Management,* Boston, MA: Harvard Business School Press, 2006, p. 84.

Chapter 2

1. Robert K. Greenleaf, *On Servant Leadership; A Journey into the Nature of Legitimate Power and Greatness,* New York, NY: Paulist Press, 2002.

2. Science Daily, *Your source for the latest research news,* n.d. Retrieved from http://www.sciencedaily.com/releases/2011/01/110121144007.htm.

3. MINDFULHUB, *Meet your Prefrontal Lobes,* June 3, 2011. Retrieved from http://mindfulhub.com.

Chapter 3

1. Cornell University, *Cornell Advanced Program for Executive Search Consulting,* 2012.

2. From the moment of contact with Zappos, I received zaps of energy and fun from every single person I connected with. Every point of contact was engaging, down to earth, and brought a smile to my often somewhat weary lips! I was lucky enough to speak with Jamie Naughton. She is their cultural

dynamo, having been with the company since 2004 and spreading the Zappos love across the world. Jamie Naughton joined Zappos.com, Inc. in 2004, right after the company relocated from the bay area to Las Vegas. As Speaker of the House, Jamie works directly with CEO Tony Hsieh (pronounced Shay), focusing on the culture. Her role is essential in creating and driving the architecture of the dynamic culture as well as focusing on culture R&D to ensure Zappos.com always stays relevant to both the employees and their customers. Jamie travels the country to work with world renowned companies, authors, researchers, and business leaders to help spread the concept that by focusing on your employees and customers, good companies can become legendary companies. Zappos.com is a leading online clothing and footwear company that has been consistently recognized as one of the best places to work. Derived from the Spanish word for shoe—zapatos—Zappos places major emphasis on company culture to achieve employee happiness and empowerment which translates into customer happiness and greater profits.

3. Tony Hsieh, "Delivering Happiness" (video), July 5, 2012. Retrieved from http://www.youtube.com/watch?v=dBKnL8Z0Xk0.

4. Donna Dickens, Buzzfeed, *27 Science Fictions that Became Science Facts in 2012,* December 19, 2012. Retrieved from http://www.buzzfeed.com/donnad/27-science-fictions-that-became-science-facts-in-2.

5. W. Brett Wilson is a Canadian leader in investment banking and investment management (FirstEnergy, Canoe Financial), an entrepreneur, and philanthropist. As a panelist on CBC's Dragon's Den for three seasons, he was known as the investor with a big heart. W. Brett Wilson, *Wikipedia, The Free Encyclopedia,* n.d. Retrieved from http://en.wikipedia.org/wiki/W._Brett_Wilson. In the late '90s Wilson, although highly successful financially, realized something fundamental was missing: "There was a huge gap between the success of my business life and the failure of my personal life." Driven to make money at the expense of his health, marriage, and children, the changes to his outlook in life did not come gently. A divorce and suffering from clinical depression were some of the manifestations of a life out of balance. Tara Henley, *Hello Canada. Hello! Entertainment, Brett Wilson,* November 1, 2012. Retrieved from http://www.wbrettwilson.ca/media-files/uploads/documents/hellocanada.pdf. Crises in his personal life however created opportunities to see himself and his life differently. Sharing custody with his ex-wife, he began to spend less time at work and more time with his children. "I stopped going into the office at 6:30 a.m. I went home for supper. I wanted the kids to understand that I was here for them. So, I was home. I didn't travel; I didn't go to charity events. If I had the kids, that was sacred. I went from zero to 60 in a week in terms of building a relationship with the kids." Tara Henley, *Hello Canada. Hello! Entertainment, Brett Wilson,* November 1, 2012. Retrieved from http://www.wbrettwilson.ca/media-files/uploads/documents/hellocanada.pdf. And

being diagnosed with cancer a few years later accentuated the need for a life overhaul. "But cancer may have saved my life. It forced me to look at everything and just say no. If not for that, I may have worked myself to death. So, I changed my priorities. If you don't have your health, you've got nothing." Tara Henley, *Hello Canada. Hello! Entertainment,* Brett Wilson, November 1, 2012. Retrieved from http://www.wbrettwilson.ca/media-files/ uploads/documents/hellocanada.pdf.

6. Shawna Guiltner is a client of BluEra. She is energetic, engaging, positive, and honest. She has 20 years sales, marketing, financial, distribution, original equipment manufacturer and general management experience in large corporate and international markets. Customer service is Shawna's top priority and she is well-known in the industry for providing a balanced approach to a range of process solutions.

7. Kolin Lymworth, Banyen's founder and still current owner, understands that we are in the process of a great transformation of life through the spirit in its many forms. Unlike today, in 1970, books about the spiritual path were relatively few or hard to come by. Since that time, it has been Kolin's and Banyen's goal to provide education and nourishment for the human soul and community in the form of books, music, videos, talks, workshops, performances, and other events, as well as Banyen's own publications. Despite the challenges faced by bookstores currently, with over 27,000 volumes under its roof, Banyen still sells over 6,000 books a month.

8. http://www.youtube.com/watch?v=dBKnL8Z0Xk0).

9. Rich Thompson, "For a More Flexible Workforce, Hire Self-Aware People." *Harvard Business Review Blogs.* Hiring, January 10, 2014. Retrieved from http://blogs.hbr.org/2014/01/for-a-more-flexible-workforce-hire-self-aware-people/.

10. Ernst & Young, *Groundbreakers: Using the strength of women to rebuild the world economy,* 2009. Retrieved from http://www.ey.com/Publication/ vwLUAssets/Groundbreakers_-_Using_the_strength_of_women_to_ rebuild_the_world_economy-new-/$FILE/Groundbreakers_Gender_report_ launched_at_Davos_Jan_09.pdf.

11. Ibid.

Chapter 4

1. Sigal Barsade and Olivia O'Neill, "Managing People. Employees Who Feel Love Perform Better," *Harvard Business Review Blogs,* January 13, 2014. Retrieved from http://blogs.hbr.org/2014/01/employees-who-feel-love-perform-better/.

2. James L. Heskett, Thomas O. Johnes, Gary W. Loveman, W. Earl Sasser Jr., and Leonard Schlesinger, "Putting the Service Profit Chain to Work," *Harvard Business Review,* March-April, 2004.

3. Ray Hemachandra, "Eckhart Tolle on making money, alignment with life, and the present moment," September 25, 2010. Retrieved from http://rayhemachandra.com/2010/09/25/eckhart-tolle-on-making-money/.

4. "100 Best Companies to Work For. Zappos.com," *Fortune,* 2013. Retrieved from http://money.cnn.com/magazines/fortune/best-companies/2013/snapshots/31.html.

5. Rob Pockar is the CEO of Matrix Solutions Inc., an employee-owned environmental and engineering consulting company. His company focuses on finding environmentally sound solutions for their government and business clients. Pockar believes that many of society's problems will be solved with science-based solutions, "whether that's economics, whether it's social science, whether it's biology or meteorology." He believes that a greater appreciation of science is necessary for all of us to be good stewards of the Earth. Along with greater scientific literacy and scientific curiosity, Pockar believes that society needs to be "awake and humble". Self-awareness and humility are recurring themes for Pockar.

6. Zappos Insights. *Culture Q & A,* n.d. Retrieved from http://www.zapposinsights.com/qa.

7. Zappos Insights. *Who we are. The Zappos Insights Team,* n.d. Retrieved from http://www.zapposinsights.com/about/who-we-are.

8. Zappos. *Wikipedia, The Free Encyclopedia,* n.d. Retrieved from http://en.wikipedia.org/wiki/Zappos.

9. Harish Hande, "Harish Hande: India Can Show The Right Way To Do Business," Features/Third Anniversary Special, *Forbes India,* May 19, 2012. Retrieved from http://forbesindia.com/article/third-anniversary-special/harish-hande-india-can-show-the-right-way-to-do-business/32936/1.

10. Northland Corporation is fortunate to have a team that averages over 20 years of tenure for salaried staff and a great group of hourly employees, many of which have been with the company for decades. http://www.northlandcorp.com/.

Chapter 5

1. Dr. Barling taught me leadership and Human Resources Management during my MBA at Queen's in the early 2000's. Dr. Barling holds the Borden Chair of Leadership at Queen's School of Business. He is an authority on

transformational leadership, and has received numerous awards for both research and teaching, including the National Post's "Leaders in Business Education" award. He was elected as a fellow of the Royal Society of Canada, and named a Queen's Research Chair in 2002. He has been elected a fellow of the Society for Industrial and Organizational Psychology, the European Academy of Occupational Health Psychology, the Association for Psychological Sciences, and the Canadian Psychological Association. He is the author of 175 articles and 10 books, including the *Handbook of Organizational Behavior*, the *Handbook of Work Stress*, and the *Handbook of Workplace Violence*. His most recent book is *The Science of Leadership: Lessons from Research for Organizational Leaders* that Forbes Magazine rated as one of the most creative books of 2014.

2. Tony Schwartz and Christine Porath, "Why You Hate Work", *The New York Times, Opinion,* May 30, 2014. Retrieved from http://mobile.nytimes.com/2014/06/01/opinion/sunday/why-you-hate-work.html?smid=tw-nytimes&_r=1&referrer=.

3. Rose Marcario is the president and CEO of Patagonia and Patagonia Works. Rose came to Patagonia with 15 years' experience in corporate finance and global operations, including as executive vice president in charge of mergers, acquisitions, and private placements for Los Angeles-based Capital Advisors and senior vice president and CFO of General Magic (a spin-off of Apple Computer, Inc.). She serves on the Board of Trustees for Naropa University (a Buddhist liberal arts college in Boulder, Colorado) and her environmental activism includes preservation focused work with organizations like the Joshua Tree National Park Association and the Mojave Desert Land Trust. After joining Patagonia in 2008, she quickly embarked on transforming the company's infrastructure to improve its operations and financial performance in addition to broadening business throughout Europe, Japan, and Australia. Marcario has helped Patagonia focus on innovation and the development of new product groups, processes and technologies, including biorubber suits, traceable down, and full range insulation for Nano Air products.

4. Sigal Barsade and Olivia O'Neill, "Managing People. Employees Who Feel Love Perform Better," *Harvard Business Review Blogs,* January 13, 2014. Retrieved from http://blogs.hbr.org/2014/01/employees-who-feel-love-perform-better/.

5. Ibid.

6. Joel Solomon is the president of Renewal Partners and chairman of Renewal Funds. Renewal Funds builds upon almost 20 years of experience in successful high impact investing. Investing for example, in companies like Stonyfield Farms. Renewal Partners Investments, The world's largest organic yogurt maker. *Gary's Story,* n.d. Retrieved from http://www.renewalpartners.com/investments/stories/stonyfield-farm. Joel serves as a senior advisor with RSF Social Finance

and speaks frequently throughout North America, including a 2012 TEDx Vancouver talk. He is a founding member of Social Venture Network (SVN), Business for Social Responsibility (BSR), the Tides Canada Foundation, and is board chair of Hollyhock. From 1993 to 2008, Joel managed the family office activities of Carol Newell. Together, they pioneered an integrated use of capital for social impact that is now growing as a strategy for deep mission investors. Joel has received a Lifetime Achievement Award from SVN and was recently inducted with Carol Newell into the SVN Hall of Fame.

Chapter 6

1. "Evidence Supports Health Benefits of 'Mindfulness-Based Practices'". *News Wise*, Lippincott Williams & Wilkins, Wolters Kluwer, July 11, 2012. Retrieved from http://www.newswise.com/articles/evidence-supports-health-benefits-of-mindfulness-based-practices.

2. Steven Handel, *The Emotion Machine. Mindfulness and Neuroplasticity*, May 17, 2011. Retrieved from http://www.theemotionmachine.com/mindfulness-and-neuroplasticity.

3. Daniel J. Siegel, *Pocket Guide to Interpersonal Neurobiology: An Integrative Handbook of the Mind*, chapter 33-2.

4. Maria Gonzalez, "Managing yourself. Mindfulness for People Who Are Too Busy to Meditate," *Harvard Business Review*, March 31, 2014. Retrieved from http://blogs.hbr.org/2014/03/mindfulness-for-people-who-are-too-busy-to-meditate/?utm_source=Socialflow&utm_medium=Tweet&utm_campaign=Socialflow.

5. Bill George, "The Third Metric. Resilience Through Mindful Leadership," *The Huffington Post*, March 22, 2013. Retrieved from http://www.huffingtonpost.com/bill-george/resilience-through-mindfu_b_2932269.html.

6. Erik Kaae was an absolute rock star at Microsoft in Denmark. He has been actively studying the Enneagram for the last eight years. He was the SMS&P director, for Denmark and Iceland. He is known for his ability to make things happen with heart.

Chapter 7

1. Adria Vasil, "The mindful corporation," *Workplace, Corporate Knights*, April 10, 2014. Retrieved from http://www.corporateknights.com/channels/workplace/the-mindful-corporation//workplace/the-mindful-corporation/.

2. Dave Logan is the #1 New York Times bestselling author of *Tribal Leadership* and his energy is absolutely infectious. He teaches at the USC Marshall School of Business, where he's been loitering since 1996. Author of four books, consultant to three dozen Fortune 500 companies, and PhD in organizational communication from the Annenberg School at USC.

3. Mark A. Montemurro has been vice president of Thermal at Baytex Energy Corp. since November 18, 2013. Montemurro has been senior vice president of Engineering and Geosciences at Sunshine Oilsands Ltd. since April 2013. He is a co-founder of Alter NRG Corporation. He has been an Independent senior advisor for Banking & Investment Business at ThomasLloyd Group PLC since December 2011. He has held a variety of executive positions, primarily leading subsurface, facility and operations teams with Sunshine Oilsands Ltd., Laricina Energy Limited, Deer Creek Energy Limited, and PanCanadian Energy Corporation. He served as the chief executive officer of Westinghouse Plasma Corporation. He has an extensive and highly successful history in alternate/renewable energy technology development and deployment. He also has more than 30 years of oil and gas experience, focusing primarily on conventional and thermal heavy oil. He had leadership roles in commercializing innovative technology in conventional oil and gas, such as horizontal drilling.

4. MBA, *10 Big Companies that Promote Employee Meditation,* February 1, 2012. Retrieved from http://www.onlinemba.com/blog/10-big-companies-that-promote-employee-meditation/.

5. Otton Scharmer, "The Third Metric. Davos: Mindfulness, Hotspots, and Sleepwalkers," *The Huffington Post,* January 26, 2014. Retrieved from http://m.huffpost.com/us/entry/4671062.

Chapter 8

1. Tony Schwartz, "Shared Value. Companies that Practice 'Conscious Capitalism' Perform 10X Better," *Harvard Business Review,* April 4, 2013. Retrieved from http://blogs.hbr.org/2013/04/companies-that-practice-conscious-capitalism-perform/.

2. Tony Robbins, *The Wealth of Passion, Money—Master The Game.* New York, NY: Simon & Schuster, 2014, p. 576.

3. Tony Schwartz, "Shared Value. Companies that Practice 'Concious Capitalism' Perform 10X Better," *Harvard Business Review,* April 4, 2013. Retrieved from http://blogs.hbr.org/2013/04/companies-that-practice-conscious-capitalism-perform/.

Chapter 9

1. Kent Brown is my (Catherine) husband and lifelong partner. We have been together since I was 17. We have raised two boys together, John and Michael. Kent led Canada's largest renewable energy company, Canadian Hydro Developers, which was taken over by another power company. He has now started another renewable energy company, BluEarth Renewables Inc. He and his team are known to be the renewable energy leaders in Canada. He was named Canadian Innovator of the Year from Clean Energy Canada in 2014.

2. Lydia Dishman, "Unlimited Vacation doesn't create slackers—it ensures productivity," *Fast Company,* n.d. Retrieved from http://www.fastcompany.com/1823415/unlimited-vacation-doesnt-create-slackers-it-ensures-productivity.

3. Tony Robbins, *David Swensen: A $23.9 Billion Labor of Love, Money—Master The Game,* New York, NY: Simon & Schuster, 2014, pp. 541-2.

Chapter 10

1. Tony Robbins, *The Final Secret, Money—Master the Game,* New York, NY: Simon & Schuster, 2014, p. 576.

2. Alibaba, *Alibaba Group Earmarks 0.3 Percent of Annual Revenue for Conservation of Environment,* May 16, 2010. Retrieved from http://news.alibaba.com/article/detail/alibaba/100303683-1-alibaba-group-earmarks-0.3-percent.html.

3. Bien Perez, "Alibaba founder Jack Ma to focus on mentoring," *South China Morning Post,* February 18, 2013. Retrieved from http://www.scmp.com/business/companies/article/1152686/alibaba-founder-focus-mentoring.

4. Tony Robbins, *Paul Tudor James: A Modern-Day Robin Hood, Money—Master The Game,* New York, NY: Simon & Schuster, 2014, p. 495.

5. Jake Richardson, *Delivering Happiness. Charity Work and Employee Satisfaction,* February 18, 2013. Retrieved from http://deliveringhappinessatwork.com/charity-work-and-employee-satisfaction/.

6. Go Overseas, *6 Companies That Will Pay You to Volunteer Abroad,* July 23, 2012. Retrieved from http://www.gooverseas.com/blog/6-companies-will-pay-volunteer-abroad.

7. Google Inc., *Great Rated,* October 1, 2014. Retrieved from http://us.greatrated.com/google-inc.

8. Google Blog, *GoogleServe 2013. Giving back on a global scale,* June 28, 2013. Retrieved from http://googleblog.blogspot.ca/2013/06/googleserve-2013-giving-back-on-global.html.

9. Delivering Happiness, *Charity Work and Employee Satisfaction,* n.d. Retrieved from http://deliveringhappinessatwork.com/charity-work-and-employee-satisfaction/.

10. Free the Children, *Our Story,* n.d. Retrieved from http://www.freethechildren.com/about-us/our-story/.

11. Tony Robbins, *Paul Tudor James: A Modern-Day Robin Hood, Money— Master The Game,* New York, NY: Simon & Schuster, 2014, p. 489.

12. Me to We, *A Family of Organizations,* n.d. Retrieved from http://www.metowe.com/about-us/a-family-of-organizations/.

13. Me to We, *Our Story. The Story of Me to We,* n.d. Retrieved from http://www.metowe.com/about-us/our-story/.

14. Me to We, *Environmental Impacts,* n.d. Retrieved from http://www.metowe.com/wp-content/external/flipbook/impact_report/#10.

15. Selco, *About Us,* n.d. Retrieved from http://www.selco-india.com/about_us.html.

16. Harish Hande, "Harish Hande: India Can Show The Right Way To Do Business," Features/Third Anniversary Special, *Forbes India,* May 19, 2012. Retrieved from http://forbesindia.com/article/third-anniversary-special/harish-hande-india-can-show-the-right-way-to-do-business/32936/1

Chapter 11

1. Gar Alperovitz, "The New-Economy Movement," *The Nation,* May 25, 2011. Retrieved from http://www.thenation.com/article/160949/new-economy-movement#.

2. Henry Mintzbery, *Rebalancing Society,* n.d. Retrieved from http://www.mintzberg.org/sites/default/files/page/rebalancing_basic_point.pdf.

3. Harish Hande, "Harish Hande: India Can Show The Right Way To Do Business," Features/Third Anniversary Special, *Forbes India,* May 19, 2012. Retrieved from http://forbesindia.com/article/third-anniversary-special/harish-hande-india-can-show-the-right-way-to-do-business/32936/1.

4. Ibid.

5. Ibid.

Chapter 13

1. Lynne Twist, "Lynne Twist—Quotes," *Good Reads,* n.d. Retrieved from http://www.goodreads.com/author/quotes/108116.Lynne_Twist.

2. Physics Central, "How much of the human body is made up of stardust?" n.d. Retrieved from http://www.physicscentral.com/explore/poster-stardust.cfm.

Chapter 14

1. James L. Heskett, Thomas O. Johnes, Gary W. Loveman, W. Earl Sasser Jr., and Leonard Schlesingerm, "Putting the Service Profit Chain to Work," *Harvard Business Review,* March-April 2004.

2. Marcus Buckingham and Curt Coffman, *First, Break All the rules: What the World's Greatest Managers Do Differently,* 1999, p. 33. New York: Simon and Schuster,

3. Tom Rath, and James K. Harter, *Well Being: The Five Essential Elements,* New York, NY: Gallup Press, 2010, p. 26.

4. Tony Robbins, *Mary Callahan Erodes: The Trillion Dollar Woman: Money— Master The Game,* New York, NY: Simon & Schuster, 2014, p. 501.

5. Ibid.

6. Thich Nhat Hanh, *You Are Here,* Boston, MA: Shambahala, 2010. p. 106.

7. Florian Heiner quotes are from an interview conducted by my editor at Namaste Publishing, David Robert Ord.

8. Ubuntu (philosophy), *Wikipedia The Free Encyclopedia,* n.d. Retrieved from http://en.wikipedia.org/wiki/Ubuntu_(philosophy).

9. Emma Seppala, "The Compassionate Mind," *Psychological Science. Observer,* n.d. Retrieved from http://www.psychologicalscience.org/index.php/publications/observer/2013/may-june-13/the-compassionate-mind.html.

10. Sage Publications, *Compassion Training Alters Altruism and Neural. Responses to Suffering,* n.d. Retrieved from http://pss.sagepub.com/content/early/2013/05/20/0956797612469537.abstract.

11. Tony Schwartz, "Shared Value. Companies that Practice 'Conscious Capitalism' Perform 10X Better," *Harvard Business Review,* April 4, 2013. Retrieved from http://blogs.hbr.org/2013/04/companies-that-practice-conscious-capitalism-perform/.

Chapter 16

1. Industry Canada, "Archived—Profile of Growth Firms: A Summary of Industry Canada Research, SME Research and Statistics," n.d. Retrieved from http://www.ic.gc.ca/eic/site/061.nsf/eng/h_rd02278.html.

2. Scott A. Shane, *The Illusions of Entrepreneurship: The Costly Myths that Entrepreneurs, Investors, and Policymakers Live By*, New Haven: Yale University Press, 2008.

3. Tony Schwartz and Christine Porath, "Why You Hate Work," *The New York Times*, n.d. Retrieved from http://mobile.nytimes.com/2014/06/01/opinion/sunday/why-you-hate-work.html?smid=tw-nytimes&_r=1&referrer=.

4. Aaron C.H. Schat, Michael R. Frone, Kevin E. Kelloway, Kevin E. Barling, Julian Hurrell, J. Joseph, Jr., "Prevalence of Workplace Aggression in the US Workforce, Findings From a National Study," *Handbook of Workplace Violence*, Thousand Oaks, CA: Sage, 2006.

5. Ibid.

6. John Aiden Byrne, "New High Finance," *New York Post*, March 17, 2013. Retrieved from (http://www.nypost.com/p/news/business/new_high_finance_gF1594vGbhI1i0FYSliCBL.

7. McKinsey & Company, *Insights & Publications*, n.d. Retrieved from http://www.mckinsey.com/insights/organization/organizational_health_the_ultimate_competitive_advantage.

8. Ibid.

9. Patrick Lencioni, *The Advantage. Why Organizational Health Trumps Everything Else in Business*, San Francisco, CA: Jossey Bass, 2012, p. 4.

10. Social Wellness, *The Impact of Social Isolation*, n.d. Retrieved from http://socialwellness.wordpress.com/the-causes-and-impact-of-social-isolation/.

11. You can see Genius Hour at the following link: Grade6ep. *Change the World: Start with you. What is Genius Hour All About?* n.d. http://grade6ep.weebly.com/what-is-genius-hour.html.

12. "Unfairness and health: evidence from the Whitehall II Study," *Journal of Epidemiology & Community Health*. Retrieved from http://www.ncbi.nlm.nih.gov/pmc/articles/PMC2465722/#ref10.

Chapter 17

1. Jeff Rubin, *The End of Growth*, Toronto, ON: Vintage Canada, 2012, p. 275.

2. Matthew and Terces Engelhart, "Mindful Culture through Simple Exercises," *Harvard Business. Review Blog,* January 20, 2104. Retrieved from http://blogs.hbr.org/2014/01/mindful-culture-through-simple-exercises/?utm_source=Socialflow&utm_medium=Tweet&utm_campaign=Socialflow.

3. Jeffrey Pfeffer, and Robert Sutton, *Hard Facts, Dangerous Half Truths & Total Nonsense, Profiting from Evidence Based Management,* Boston, MA: Harvard, 2006, p. 81.

4. Ibid., p. 133.

5. Julian Barling, *The Science of Leadership: Lessons from Research for Organizational Leaders,* New York, NY: Oxford Press, 2014, p. 207.

ABOUT THE AUTHOR AND COLLABORATORS

Catherine R. Bell draws on her experience of merging the paths of executive search and team transformation with various wisdom traditions and practices that cultivate presence (deep self-awareness). She emphasizes how important and relevant the cultivation of basic presence or mindfulness combined with self awareness is for the development of executives and companies so they can navigate and adapt to the modern world of rapid change and rapid response. In doing so, she has helped some of the world's Fortune 500 companies and entrepreneurs grow more consciously. She is the Co-Founder of BluEra. She has a degree in Sociology from the Western University, and an MBA from Queen's University. She is certified in the Enneagram from the Enneagram Institute in New York, and has completed an extensive course in Executive Search from Cornell University. She has completed hundreds of searches and BluEra has been recognized as one of Alberta's best workplaces. She is also a certified yoga instructor. She also led the initiatives of BluBoards, which involves her company giving back to the non-profit community. She has been involved in a number of not for profit Boards, most recently, The Distress Centre, which helps some of the most vulnerable populations. She is married to Kent Brown, who is also an entrepreneur, and has two thriving boys, John and Michael Brown.

This book has been midwifed by Russ Hudson and Christopher Papadopoulos.

Russ Hudson is one of the principal scholars and innovative thinkers in the Enneagram world today. He has been teaching internationally for the last two decades and has "rock star" status in the spiritual community. He has coached both business teams and leaders in business thought. He is Executive Director of Enneagram Personality Types, Inc. and co-Founder of The Enneagram Institute. He has been co-leading a spiritual business for years and believes in the importance of ongoing transformation. He has been co-teaching the Enneagram Professional Training Programs since 1991, and is a Founding Director and former Vice-President of the International Enneagram Association. He is also co-author of *The Wisdom of the Enneagram, Personality Types* (Revised Edition), *Understanding the Enneagram* (Revised Edition), *Discovering Your Personality Type* (Revised Edition), and *The Power of the Enneagram* (audio CD). He also assisted Don Riso in writing *Enneagram Transformations*. He holds a degree in East Asian Studies from Columbia University in New York, from which he graduated Phi Beta Kappa. Catherine, Russ, and Christopher have combined wisdom from the Enneagram (please see www.enneagraminstitute.com) and various other business, spiritual, and psychological traditions to help organizations flourish.

Christopher Papadopoulos is a teacher of present moment awareness, who in 2003 experienced a permanent shift in consciousness from mind identification to the peace and clarity of Now. For the past decade he has helped individuals discover that behind their thoughts and emotions lies their true, peaceful self. His book, *Peace—And Where To Find It,* reveals that deep body awareness quiets our mind activity and enables the awareness and experience of our truly wise, peaceful nature.

namaste PUBLISHING · books that change your life

Our Service Territory Expands

Since introducing Eckhart Tolle to the world with *The Power of Now* in 1997 (followed by *Stillness Speaks, A New Earth,* and *Milton's Secret*), NAMASTE PUBLISHING has been committed to bringing forward only the most evolutionary and transformational publications that acknowledge and encourage us to awaken to who we truly are: spiritual beings of inestimable value and creative power.

In our commitment to expand our service purpose—indeed, to redefine it—we have created a unique website that provides a global spiritual gathering place to support and nurture individual and collective evolution in consciousness. You will have access to our publications in a variety of formats: traditional books, eBooks, audiobooks, CDs, and DVDs. Increasingly, our publications are available for instant download.

We invite you to get to know our authors by going to their individual pages on the website. We also invite you to read our blogs: The Compassionate Eye, Consciousness Rising, Conscious Parenting, and Health. Enjoy the wisdom of Bizah, a lovable student of Zen, presented in daily and weekly entries.

We are each in our different ways both teachers and students. For this reason, the Namaste spiritual community provides an opportunity to meet other members of the community, share your insights, update your "spiritual status," and contribute to our online spiritual dictionary.

We also invite you to sign up for our free ezine Namaste Insights, which is packed with cutting edge articles on spirituality, many of them written by leading spiritual teachers. The ezine is only available electronically and is not produced on a set schedule.

What better way to experience the reality and benefits of our oneness than by gathering in spiritual community? Tap into the power of collective consciousness and help us bring about a more loving world.

We request the honor of your presence at
www.namastepublishing.com